going the distance

The Keswick Year Book 2012

going the distance

Living in the Light of the Future

Simon Manchester
Christopher Ash
Mike Raiter
Chris Sinkinson
Dominic Smart
Calisto Odede
Ian Coffey

First published 2013

British Library Cataloguing in Publication Data
A catalogue record for this book is available from the British Library.

ISBN: 978–1–84474–840–2

Set in Dante 12.5/16pt
Typeset in Great Britain by CRB Associates, Potterhanworth, Lincolnshire
Printed and bound in Great Britain by Ashford Colour Press Ltd, Gosport, Hampshire

Contents

Introduction by the Chairman of the 2012 Convention

It seems likely that memories of summer 2012 will linger in our minds for many years to come. From the celebration of the Queen's Diamond Jubilee, through the spectacular success of the Olympic Games to the inspirational achievements of the Paralympians, this was a summer that has left its mark on both our national life and on global sporting history.

The message of Keswick 2012 could hardly have fitted better into such a summer. 'Going the Distance' was a call to Christian perseverance, a call to keep running the race of Christian discipleship set before us in the face of personal struggle, spiritual attack and secular opposition. It was, from beginning to end, a Convention to remember, with faithful and powerful preaching, stirring praise and worship and rich Christian fellowship.

In this selection of some of the most memorable moments of Keswick 2012, Simon Manchester helps us to listen in on Jesus' call to his disciples to persevere in a challenging world after he has returned to the Father. The evening talks also take us from Genesis to Revelation, through the searching challenges of some of Jesus' parables about his return, and into the mysteries of the book of Ecclesiastes. It is a rich feast indeed and our prayer is that this book will bring its riches to a wider audience for the glory of our Lord Jesus and the blessing of his people as we continue to run the race for his glory.

John Risbridger
Chairman

The Bible Readings

Prepared for a New Day: John 14 – 17

by Simon Manchester

Simon is Rector of St Thomas' North Sydney. He heard the message of his sin and Christ's forgiveness in his last year of school, believing it to be the best message in the world, and he still does! Simon has been married to Kathy since 1975 and they have three children – Rachel, Beth and Samuel.

1. Crucial Answers: John 14:1–14

Well, dear friends, it's a great pleasure to be with you. I am hoping that these studies will help you focus on Jesus Christ, that he will impress you more and that you will be devoted to him as a result. We've chosen chapters which I know are extremely familiar and I hope that there was no one who groaned when you saw we were going to do John 14 – 17 because these chapters of Scripture are like the Pacific Ocean: they can be searched forever.

We need John 14 – 17 for a number of reasons. First of all, as you read these chapters you realize that there is somebody called the Lord Jesus who is able to look all the difficulties and hostilities of the world in the face and be completely in charge and calm. We also need these chapters because they are very reassuring. We are sinful people, we look good in a convention, we are saints and we're sinners, we are fitful, we are feeble, we are inconsistent and yet we have this wonderful, faithful, totally in charge, totally steadfast, loving Saviour. We also need the supernaturalism of these chapters. John 14 – 17 give us crucial teaching on the person of the Holy Spirit who leads us, not randomly into strange paths, but into the very paths of the Scriptures to the Son of God that we would trust and obey him more.

We are going to look this morning at verses 1–14. We tend to hear these verses at a funeral and they look as though they are just the beginning of a conversation. But, actually, they are a response to Peter who says things in chapter 13 which Jesus takes up. I want you, therefore, to picture Jesus sitting with the disciples and they've just finished the last supper. There are three disciples around the table – Peter, Thomas, and Philip – who all say stupid things and Jesus wonderfully brings the subject back to himself. Peter says something that is odd to Jesus, Thomas says something that is nervous to Jesus, Philip says something which is unhelpful to Jesus. That's why I have called this section, 'Crucial Answers'.

Peter's self-confidence

John 13:33 says: 'My children, I will be with you only a little longer. You will look for me, and just as I told the Jews, so I tell you now: where I am going, you cannot come.' Jesus has just washed their feet, they have had their meal and Judas has left. Jesus says that he's leaving, they are not coming on this particular journey, they are going to stay and they are going to love each other, but Peter doesn't seem to listen. Now, friends, what do you say when someone says to you, 'I am going to die; three days later I am going to rise'? The normal thing would be to say, 'Sorry, could you say that again?' or 'How are you going to do this? It's OK if you are going to die as long as you are going to rise.' But Peter doesn't listen, he just hears Jesus say he will die. And here Jesus says he's going to go away, and Peter's reaction is, 'You shouldn't be leaving. I'm unhappy that you are leaving.' The reply comes back in verse 36, 'Where I am going, you cannot follow now, but you will follow later.' And Peter says, 'No, I can follow now; in fact, I'll die for you, that's how capable I am.' Jesus replies immediately, John 14:1: 'Do not let your hearts be troubled. You believe in God; believe also in me. My Father's house has many rooms.' Do you see what Jesus is doing? 'Peter, you are not that brave, you are not going to be that successful, you are not worth trusting, trust in me.' That is why Jesus questions the boast of Peter as he speaks up for himself, and he instructs the disciples and all of us who are here today to trust him and not ourselves. Jesus is saying, 'I'm not inferior to God; your trust is in God, your trust should be in me.'

Peter says, 'You can trust me, Jesus!' Jesus says, 'No, you need to trust me.' Please notice in passing that the answer to Peter's bravado and their anxiety – because they do have troubled hearts – is that Jesus wants them to put their trust in a well-placed object. And the well-placed object is himself. He wants them to place their trust in someone who can deal with the fear and with the future and that is himself. And what Jesus is doing in these very wonderful verses is dealing with the long-term problem they have, which is how is anybody going to get from here to heaven? After, of course, he will deal with the short-term problem of how the disciples are going to live in the world. He will tell of how the Holy Spirit will come to equip and enable, but at the moment he is talking about his leaving for the long-term solution of getting them to glory.

And I want you to listen very carefully to this. How is Jesus going to secure the long-term future for those who believe? The answer he says is, 'I go to prepare a place for you.' Now we completely miss the point if we think that Jesus means I go *up* to prepare a place for you. I don't like to point out where a text or translation is not helpful but the NIV has stuck a word into verse 2 which doesn't help and shouldn't be there and it's the little word, 'there'. Jesus says, 'I am going to prepare a place for you,' but the NIV says, 'I am going *there* to prepare a place for you.' And so most people mistakenly think that Jesus is saying, 'I am going to *heaven* to prepare a place for you,' that is, 'I am going to heaven and I am going to get out a hammer, a saw, nails and some wallpaper and I am going to prepare a place for you.' But Jesus is not saying that. He's saying, 'I am going *out* to prepare a place for you. I am not going *up* to prepare a place for you. I am going *out* to prepare a place for you. I am going out of this room, I will be going out of the city and when I am on the cross I am going to be out of fellowship with the Father. And because I am going out of the room, out of the city and out of the Father's fellowship, you can go in. Because I get the exit, you get the entrance; because I get banished, you get welcomed.' It's exactly the same in that lovely passage in Mark 15 when Jesus cries out, 'My God, my God, why have you forsaken me?' and the curtain suddenly splits down the middle. There is Jesus crying on the cross and God says to him, 'Get out,' and at that very moment the curtain splits down the middle, and God says to everybody that has got two ears, 'Come in.'

Now because I prepare a place, says Jesus, 'I will come and I'll take you to be with me.' And, friends, let me remind you that the definition of heaven is to be with Jesus. If your concept of heaven is not a concept where Jesus is central you may be inventing something which has to do with family, reunions, happiness, golf courses, pubs and fishing. But actually what is going to make heaven, is that we will be with Jesus. When Jesus is present and removes all the evil, all the sadness and all the suffering and includes all the blessing, all the love, all the truth and all the security, that's heaven, and we must have a Christ-centred view of heaven.

Jesus is speaking to the disciples who are troubled but he wants them to be extremely sure, so he says these lovely words in verse 2, 'If it were not so I would have told you.' 'If it were not like this you can be sure I would have filled you in,' says Jesus. 'But it is like this and that's why I'm telling you. I go, I prepare, I'll come, I'll take, I'll be your destination, I, I, I – trust me. I'll do this, not you, Peter.'

Now I think it's unlikely that Peter grasped this. One of the reasons I think that Peter denied Jesus is not that he was cowardly at that particular moment when he was asked about whether he knew Jesus. I suspect that when Peter was arrested his self-confident theology was starting to unravel. Whatever views he had about Jesus bringing some immediate hope and success were starting to unravel quite badly and I wonder whether Peter didn't find himself saying, 'I'm not sure that I should align myself with this man.' It doesn't strike me as if Peter is a cowardly man. He gets his sword out in the garden, he's quite a bold man, he's quite an upfront man, he says what he thinks, he does what he likes. But Peter seems to have a theological problem which is, that if Jesus is going to die on purpose, something has gone wrong. He can't cope with this idea that Jesus would die on purpose. I suspect that Peter distances himself from Jesus because he realizes that whatever is going on, he doesn't really understand it. In other words, I think that Peter's problem is not as much moral as theological. And in this passage his problem is again theological. He thinks that salvation is something which is going to be partly his work; it's a DIY, do-it-yourself type of thing. If you are a DIY type of Christian and you hugely depend on yourself you will lurch between pride and being miserable. And if you are that sort of person, and perhaps there is a little bit of this in all of us, you need to get back and say, 'It's going to be him who will do the work, he will be the Saviour, he will carry me through, it's him I should be trusting and there should be less focus on me and much more on him.'

Thomas's despair

The second person who speaks up is Thomas. If Peter is self-confident, Thomas is almost the opposite. Interesting to have these people sitting round the table, isn't it? Thomas is desperate. He blurts out in chapter 14:5, 'We don't know where you are going, so how can we know the way?' And Jesus must recognize that explaining the crucifixion is too difficult for the disciples to understand, so instead he says, 'I want you to trust *me*, the person. Let's just concentrate on *me*. Let's not talk so much about atonement, redemption, reconciliation. Let's talk about trusting *me*.' And he comes back with these famous words in verse 6, 'I am the way and the truth and the life.' Thomas is not asking Jesus at the last supper if there are many ways to God. We often use John 14:6 to answer the idea that there might be many ways to God. This verse says there aren't many ways to God, Jesus is the way. But Thomas is not asking that question; Thomas is asking if there is *any* way. And Jesus says, 'I am the way and the truth and the life.'

This is the sixth time that Jesus uses the little phrase, 'I am', in John's Gospel. It is a very loaded sentence. 'I am' is a derivative of Yahweh, Jehovah, and, therefore, Jesus is using a quite explosive phrase when he describes himself again and again as 'I am'. And then he also attaches a highly significant metaphor. So when he says, 'I am the Bread,' or

'I am the Shepherd,' there are huge Old Testament implications. And here he says, 'I am the way.' Thomas says, 'We don't know the way,' and Jesus says, 'I am the way.' The whole conversation is going in this particular direction because the disciples are not able to go the way of the cross, but they need to trust the One who is the way.

They can trust Jesus who identifies himself as the way because he goes on to say that out of him comes the truth. He is trustworthy, he is reliable, and also what flows from him is the life that is forever, that is unbreakable. Jesus then says to Thomas in John 14:7, 'If you really know me, you will know my Father as well.' Now it is an amazing thing that Jesus says to Thomas, and it's one of the things that keep me going as a Christian. I go back to the New Testament and I see these remarkable phrases that Jesus uses that just cannot be said by a person who is insane or by somebody who is evil. They must be said by someone who is seeing himself, rightly, to be on a par with the God of heaven. And Jesus says to Thomas, quite simply, that if he knows him he knows the Father.

Well, if Jesus and the Father are the same, Jesus is not inferior to the Father. These very comforting verses are significant because even though Jesus is speaking to people who are deeply, deeply distressed he has even more distress on his plate, and yet he is concerned for them. Here was Jesus about to face the judgment and wrath of the Father, and he has this tremendous concern for the distressed disciples around the table. He is going to meet all their needs – in the long-term as well as the short-term.

Despite not primarily dealing with the question of whether there are many ways to God, John 14:6 does stand in the face of plural religions. And so our response to this issue must be what has been called the 'all-tolerance'. The all-tolerance says, 'I will love you whatever you say or do. I may disagree completely with what you are saying but I will keep being patient, I will keep being kind and I will stay with you.' The new-tolerance says, 'I will love you as long as we can both agree that whatever we say is all true.' We need to get back to the all-tolerance: love for people, disagreement on the issues. The new-tolerance: love for people, conditional on agreeing that everything can be true, is totally confusing our world and our church. And when Jesus speaks here in John 14:6 and says, 'I am the way and the truth and the life. No one comes to the Father but through me,' it is being said by the most loving person in the universe. This is the person who can see more clearly, who loves more dearly and speaks so plainly because he genuinely wants people to be safe and secure.

If you are in a burning building and you happen to know that only one door is unlocked, there is nothing loving about saying to the people in the building, 'Pick your door.' The loving thing is to push people, if necessary, towards the door that will open. If you are on the *Titanic* and you happen to know that only one lifeboat has no hole in it, there is nothing loving about saying to the people on board, 'Pick your lifeboat.' The loving thing to do is to say, 'Go to that particular lifeboat,' and that is what Jesus is doing here. He's saying that he's the door, he's the lifeboat; the loving thing he's telling us is we must come to him.

Philip's dissatisfaction

Now the third person whom Jesus speaks to is Philip. Peter is over confident, Thomas is desperate and Philip's problem is that he is dissatisfied. In verse 8 Philip says, 'Lord, show us the Father and that will be enough for us.' Philip's request is: 'We just need some more information, show us the Father.' There is some sympathy for Philip saying, 'I just wish we had some more information,' but there is also a sense in which what Philip is saying is completely irresponsible. He had seen Jesus turn water into wine, heal the lame man, feed thousands, heal the blind and raise Lazarus from the dead. What Jesus has done has been extraordinary, what he says is extraordinary, but still Philip says, 'I just wish we had more information.' And I suspect that every genuine Christian at some stage says, 'I just wish I had a little more information. I just wish I had a little more experience.' And Jesus comes back and he says in these very important verses, 'Don't you know me, Philip? Anyone who has seen me has seen the Father. How can you say, "Show us the Father"? Don't you believe I am in the Father and the Father is in me? The words I say to you, I don't speak on my own authority. Rather, it is the Father living in me' (verses 9–10). So to see Jesus is to see the Father. Do you want to know what the Father is like, friends? Well, look in the Scriptures at Jesus, read the Gospels and you will see what God who runs the universe is like: he's like Jesus in the Gospels. And for those of us who are tempted to stick onto God some inappropriate character or caricature, it is a wonderful thing to go back to Jesus in the Gospels and know that that's what the God who runs the universe is like.

Is it really fair for us to expect the people who are walking the streets of Keswick to be reading the Bible? Friends, I think, in a sense it is. Because God expects all people in the world to be seekers; he's given enough information in creation and in very many other places. When a person becomes a genuine seeker they should be looking for the real facts, and if they are looking for the real facts they will go back to the eye-witness accounts. And I don't think it's too much for us to say to people, 'Although it seems a little bit absurd, you ought to be reading the Bible. Don't wait for God to speak across the sky, that's not going to happen. Don't wait for God to speak in your head, that's probably not going to happen. Why don't you go and read where God has spoken?' It's like saying, 'If a telephone rings don't stick your head in the microwave!' Which is a nice way of saying, 'If God's going to speak, why don't you go where he's speaking, which is the Bible?' That's what Jesus says here to Philip – go back to the words and go back to the works. That's why John finishes his Gospel by saying (John 20:31), 'These are written that you may believe that Jesus is the Christ . . . and that by believing have life in his name.'

And now Jesus says a remarkable thing to Philip – look at verse 10: 'The words I say to you I don't speak on my own authority. Rather, it is the Father, living in me who is . . . ' What does your version say? . . . 'doing his work'. You expect it to say, 'The words I speak are the words the Father speaks.' But he doesn't. He says, 'The words I speak are the works the Father does.' What an incredible linking of the Word of God and the work of God. 'My words,' says Jesus, 'are the Father's work. When I speak, God works. God speaks, "Let there be," and things happen. I speak, and things happen. So', Jesus says to Philip, 'believe that the Father and I are profoundly related and work together' (author's translation).

Now I don't know if you've come here particularly weary, worn and sad to this Keswick Convention. It's possible that for a long time things have been quite stale for you: prayer is difficult, reading the Bible is difficult, your own walk with Jesus is difficult, your church is difficult, your family life is difficult. Every Christian, in a sense, would like to be refreshed. Is there something I'm missing? Is there something else out there that I need? I think these verses are very important to us. I think we should be saying to God, 'If you work by your Word and I go back to your Word, would you do a new work in me? Would you just renew my trust, my belief? Would you renew my repentance? Would you renew my obedience? Would you renew my fellowship? Would you renew my usefulness?' It's not a bad thing for us to go back to the God who works by his Word and to say to him, 'As I read your Word would you help me, because left to myself, I'm going nowhere?'

So Jesus says in verse 10, 'Go back to my words and stay with the words asking God to work', and verse 11: 'Go back to the works, which will encourage you that Jesus is who he said he is' (author's translation). Ask yourself as you read the words of God, 'Why are these words so powerful?' And then ask yourself, 'Why are these works that Jesus did so powerful?' It must be because he is the one he says he is. So I'm going to keep trusting him. We know that words don't convert people: we know they point people, they are a signpost to people but when people are looking or listening humbly they guide you. If a person is looking at the miracles and reading the words of Jesus with a humble heart and a genuine prayer God will do his refreshing work.

You haven't missed out on anything; there is no Christian who has more than you. You have all the riches of Christ Jesus. You have the Scriptures, same as anybody in the world; the Holy Spirit is your teacher. We need simply to learn from this anguished conversation with Philip, who's longing for more, to go back to what you've got and ask God to work with the Word that he has given you.

Well now, friends, verse 12 looks like an exaggeration, doesn't it? 'Very truly I tell you, whoever believes in me will do the works I've been doing and they will do even greater things than these because I am going to the Father.' If you have faith in Jesus, he says, you 'will do greater things'. And if the *greater* means doing better things than Jesus, how can he be serious? Am I really going to turn more water into wine? Am I really going to feed more people with a few loaves and fishes? Am I really going to bring more Lazaruses out of the graves? Impossible! What Jesus means very simply is that you are going to do greater things in eternity. You are going to do greater quality things. Those of you who put your trust in me, you are going to point people to me! You are not going to point people to a loaf of bread but to the Bread of Life. You are going to send people not just to a little lampstand but to the Light of the World. You are not going to offer people resuscitation on a hospital bed but the resurrection that outlasts the world. You are going to do greater things which all the miracles in John's Gospel were pointing to – you are going to point people to Jesus. And you are going to do this by asking him for help which is what the following verse says, 'And I'll do what you ask in my name so the Father may be glorified.'

Well, if that seems ridiculous we can only say that Jesus is a trustworthy Saviour. He means what he says and he says what he means. And because he's going to the Father, he says, 'You may ask me for anything in my name and I will do it' (verse 14). He is caught up in the context of this ministry and he's talking about helping people to come to him. That's what he delights to do.

So, friends, can you see the genius of Jesus dealing with these three men around the table? They are in various dangers and these dangers apply to us. It may be possible that there are people here in this meeting this morning and you have a little bit of Peter's self-confidence which is dangerous, or you have a little bit of Thomas's despair, or perhaps you have a little bit of Philip's dissatisfaction. And what the Lord Jesus is saying to you is trust *me*, trust *me*, trust *me*. You are in danger of leaning on yourself, trust me. You think there is no hope, trust me. You think you need more information, trust me; you've got enough. And the future is totally solved for us because, says Jesus, 'I go to prepare a place for you.' And he did go, he did go out and you will go in. He did it!

I hope as you see this phrase, 'Going the distance', you will say to yourself, 'You know, the wonderful thing about going the distance is that that's what Jesus did. He went through with the crucifixion, he went the distance and you know what? He sits on the throne of heaven, he hears my prayers, he gives me his promises and they will enable me to go the distance.' Trust him.

2. Another Counsellor: John 14:15–31

Now this morning we come to famous verses where Jesus begins to introduce the third person of the Trinity, the Holy Spirit. If Jesus' work on the cross is utterly sufficient for our eternal security, and it is, what I hope we will see in John 14 – 16 is that the work of the Holy Spirit is utterly sufficient for our usefulness, our fruitfulness and our joy in the world. Jesus did not make a mistake – he has not left us with insufficient security in the long-term or help in the short-term. The work he has done on the cross has guaranteed our long-term security and the gift of the Holy Spirit is going to enable us in the short-term. We have not been short-changed by our God.

There are five little tutorials or seminars that take place in John 14 – 16. The first is that the Holy Spirit comes to indwell the believer forever. The second is that he teaches the believer all he or she needs to know for faith and faithfulness. The third is that he helps the believer and the church in its witness. The fourth tutorial is that he convicts the world so that it begins to respond as God determines. The fifth tutorial is that all the glory goes to Jesus.

The greater life

We're looking at tutorials one and two this morning. Firstly, the Spirit is in us forever (verses 15–24). Remember that Jesus had said his disciples would do 'greater things' (John 14:12). Jesus had to teach the people that the *greater thing* was himself. Even in John 6 they got it wrong, didn't they? They were coming for bread, for food, and he had to say to them, 'No, the greater thing is me.' There is something greater than food, there is something greater than having eyes to see, there's something greater than being able to walk, there's something greater than being given a new lease of life and that is to come to the Bread of Life, to the Light of the World, to the risen Lord, the Resurrection and the Life, to come to *him* is the greater thing.

Now, friends, we are involved in helping people come to the greater life. And if we are involved in helping people to eat, see, live, get well, we can't stop there, can we? We want to be on eternal business, which is to see people come to Jesus. Of course, this eternal mission is completely beyond us, which is why Jesus says, 'You must speak to me about this and ask me for help because you are not able to do this yourself.' I imagine there are many people here this morning who are saying, 'Well, here we have another Keswick speaker telling us that we should ask and it will happen.' And you want to say, 'Mr Speaker, we don't actually believe that because we've tried asking and we don't get what we asked for. We've been doing this for a very long time and we've not been receiving what we've been asking.'

Deathless prayers

But just before you give up on these verses see that John14:14 says, 'You may ask me for anything in my name, and I will do it.' Remember when you send up your prayer and you ask God to work you are not asking for some small-scale system to get to work. The great privilege of being able to speak to our heavenly Father who runs the cosmos and eternity is that we are sending up our prayers as best we can, with the best will in the world, but we are hugely limited as to what God is actually doing. So when we pray it's not as if we are just calling a plumber expecting him to come that day. It's not as though we are putting money in a machine expecting to get a coke can back in the next sixty seconds. God *may* do amazingly speedy things and we love it when he does. But we also need to remember that when we pray to our Father we are putting our requests to somebody who is organizing an eternal, cosmic, majestic, huge plan. And if we ask how God is going to be glorified (verse 13), it may be that it is not going to be via a fast answer. It may be that God will be glorified through a long, brilliant process. God hears every prayer that is uttered, not one of them gets lost. As the puritans said, 'The prayer of the believer is deathless.' God hears our prayers better than a parent hears the cry of a child, but the whole process of his genius, all the machinery of heaven and all the processes of eternity are being worked out by this great heavenly Father, so don't be too impatient.

Can you imagine what it would have been like if Jacob had prayed for his son Joseph to come back *that day* and got his prayer answered? What a tragedy! I wouldn't have been surprised if Jacob didn't pray, 'Heavenly Father, please bring my boy Joseph back. I don't know what's happened to him, please bring him back today.' And this great, loving, majestic God says, 'You have absolutely no idea what I'm going to do. I will bring him back but it's going to be a long and most fruitful path. When he eventually does come back astronomical things will have been done.' So don't lose heart when you pray. Jesus says in verse 15, 'If you love me, keep my commands.' I wonder whether this is the command he means. I wonder whether he means, 'I'm commanding you to keep asking me because I am going to ask the Father and he's going to give you another advocate. It's a very great task that I am leaving you to do in the world. I don't want you to forget to ask for help. Totally and brilliantly I am presenting your case in heaven and the Holy Spirit is going to help you adequately, sufficiently and wonderfully with your ministry in the world.'

Forever in you

This word 'advocate' comes five times in the New Testament – four times in these chapters of John's Gospel and once in the first letter of John. The Greek word *parakletos*, 'to be called alongside', has no real English equivalent. We will never find one word to do justice to the majestic, multiple ministry of the Holy Spirit. We know from Scripture that he teaches, he convicts, he leads, he guides, he helps, he can be grieved by us, he can be resisted by us, he can be quenched and he's a person, not a force, not an *it*. Again and again theology wins over grammar in these chapters. The word *pneuma* is a neuter word and should have a neuter preposition but it is given regularly a personal preposition because the Holy Spirit is a person. So the translators come up with words like Counsellor – that's OK; Advocate – that's OK; Helper – that's OK; Paraclete – that's OK; but none of them really does justice to the great work of the Holy Spirit.

In verse 16 we have that wonderful word 'forever'. The Holy Spirit will be with you forever. Now there must be some people here today who have asked whether the Holy Spirit has left them because of that terrible story in the Old Testament of the Holy Spirit leaving Saul, and David's desperate prayer in Psalm 51 that the Spirit would never leave him. And Jesus says that the Holy Spirit will not move in and move out, he will just move in. And he will move in and he will live with your sin until you see him face to face and then you will be sinless. Aren't you grateful for that? Aren't you grateful that when we get intoxicated with a certain sin the Holy Spirit graciously, steadily and eventually convicts us?

Verse 17 says he 'will be in you'. And although it's true he dwells in each believer, the word *you* is actually in the plural. When the King James translation disappeared and we could no longer read *thee* and *thou* we ended up with the modern *you*. We tend to read *you* as personal but here it's plural. The Holy Spirit will be in you individually and he is in you plural. That's why when we gather together we have such rich fellowship, and that's why believers who disappear from church and turn up occasionally have such impoverished Christian lives. Somebody told me the other day that the average committed Christian – this could be in Australia or in the West – attends their church nineteen out of fifty-two Sundays! No wonder we're in such trouble!

Now the world is hostile to the Spirit (verse 17). The world has no relationship to the Holy Spirit. The secular person outside this auditorium hasn't a clue what we are talking about, cannot appreciate the things of the Spirit, doesn't value the things of the Lord Jesus. It's not that we are better, it's not that we're smarter, it is by grace we have been brought to receive these good things. And don't fall for the confusion that because your neighbour says they are 'spiritual' they are alive and well; to be spiritual just means that you are needy and hungry. You are not going to be fed until you come to the Bread of Life. You are not going to be at rest until you come to Jesus. You are not going to be indwelt by God's Spirit until you belong to

Jesus. The spiritual person without Christ is dead; the Christian by the grace of God is alive. There is a massive eternal gulf between the two.

Evidence of the Holy Spirit

Now I want to ask three quick questions about the work of the Holy Spirit. This is an aside to John 14 but I think you will find it helpful. Firstly, how do you know the Holy Spirit lives in you? Is it because of your feelings? A very dangerous gauge. Is it because of your giftedness? Again, a very dangerous gauge. Is it because the fruit of the Spirit is evident in your life? A very dangerous gauge. No, in the end we are going to know that the third person of the Trinity is resident in us because of the way we see the first person of the Trinity – we call him Father (Romans 8; Galatians 4). The other way we know that the third person of the Trinity is resident in us is because we address the second person of the Trinity as Lord. 'No one can say, "Jesus is Lord," except by the Holy Spirit' (1 Corinthians 12:3). When the world looks a complete mess and you can still say, 'O sovereign, living, wonderful Lord Jesus,' that's because the Holy Spirit is resident in your life. So we know that the third person of the Trinity is resident in us because of the way we address the first and second persons of the Trinity.

Second question, is the Holy Spirit indwelling believers a New Testament experience? Or, to put it another way, did the Holy Spirit live in Old Testament believers? Some people say that Old Testament believers were regenerate and indwelt. They say, 'How could Old Testament believers have a different salvation from the New Testament? Surely what Abraham experienced is what we experience – righteous and indwelt.' Others say that Old Testament believers were regenerate but not indwelt, that is, their hearts were changed so they were appreciative and receptive, but God himself was not indwelling them. If you could put it crassly and crudely you would say that God was *on* them but not *in* them.

And some people say Old Testament believers were not regenerate or indwelt because these are New Testament blessings. And John 14:17 would be a good proof text because here Jesus seems to be announcing something new and wonderful. Jesus says to the apostles that God who has been *above* for eternity and has walked *beside* them for three years is now going to be *in* them. Now I have some sympathy with the idea that this is a New Testament experience. I wouldn't want to be categorical but it does seem to me that Jesus said the Holy Spirit would *come* when he had risen (John 7). And here in John 14:17 Jesus seems to be talking of these things as a new privilege: the sort of things that Jeremiah and Ezekiel in the Old Testament were looking forward to.

Singing and praying

The third question, perhaps a little more practical, should we pray or sing to the Holy Spirit? How does the New

Testament direct us in this? We know that the Father is the priority for prayers in the New Testament. 'Pray like this', said Jesus, 'Our Father.' We know that there are a few prayers addressed *to* Jesus in the New Testament; Stephen in Acts 7 would be a good example. The New Testament is actually silent on the subject of whether we should pray to the Holy Spirit and yet many of our hymns, old and new, do address the Holy Spirit directly. And you may be interested to know, those of you who have Anglican backgrounds, some of our liturgy addresses the Holy Spirit directly.

In an interesting book called, *Engaging with the Holy Spirit*,[1] Graham Cole raises this question and offers two very wise pieces of advice. The first is that all our prayers are to the trinitarian God so it's entirely legitimate for us to speak to God as Father, Son or Holy Spirit. He is the One God. But Graham Cole says we should aim as much as we can to indicate in our prayer life that we actually believe we are addressing the Father *through* the Son *with the help of* the Holy Spirit. This will distinguish us from a whole lot of religions which just basically call to God and, therefore, our prayer life can be an indication of the wonderful theology of the cross. I think that's very helpful.

Jesus is alive

Let's go back to the text in John 14:18. What does Jesus mean when he says, 'I will not leave you . . . I will come to you'? What are the disciples meant to conclude from that particular sentence? Does he mean, 'I am about to leave you on Friday and come back on Sunday'? Yes. Does he mean, 'I am about to leave you in forty days, fifty days, and I'll come as the Holy Spirit comes and takes residence in your life'? Yes. Does he mean, 'I am about to ascend but one day I'll return'? Yes. Which of them are the disciples meant to conclude? Well, he says in verse 19, 'You will see me,' and I guess this primarily means they will see him quite quickly at the resurrection.

Verse 19 says, 'Because I live, you also will live.' Have you ever thought about that? He lives so you who believe must live. As soon as you sent up your prayer to him for salvation he committed himself to you, Shepherd to sheep, 'I will get you home. I live, you will live.' What a wonderful promise. This is not human achievement, this is Jesus saying, 'I live; you will live.' I love the story of Spurgeon when he went to visit his orphanage. He got out a basin of water in front of the kids and he plunged his hands into the basin. He said to the boys and girls, 'Now why don't my hands drown?' And a little boy said, 'Because your head's not in the water!' That's it, isn't it? Our head, the Lord Jesus, has risen. He is alive, always alive, so we, his body, cannot die.

Eyes and ears

And in verse 20 Jesus explains that so much is going to make sense when all this takes place. 'You will realize I am in my Father, and you are in me, and I'm in you.' These disciples were very slow witted as you know; it took a long time for them to grasp many of the basic things which we read and understand today. In John 2 Jesus said, destroy this temple, I'll raise it. John says that they didn't know what he was talking about, but when the Spirit came, they got it. In John 12 Jesus rides into Jerusalem on a donkey. John says that they didn't know what this was all about, but when the Spirit came, they got it. In John 20 they go to the tomb and find it empty. John says that they did not understand, but when you look at Peter's and John's writings they are crystal clear because the resurrection has taken place; the Holy Spirit has come and they have eyes and ears to see.

Friends, if you understand Jesus died for me, that is my security for the future. Jesus lives by his Spirit in me. He is the one who will enable me to adequately, effectively live in this world; that is a miracle! The average person in this town, in this country, in this world doesn't understand that. It's not that they are worse than us, it's not that they are dumber than us, it's that God has been so merciful and has opened blind eyes, deaf ears and given us grace to grasp all the relationships – Father, Son, and Holy Spirit. Belonging to the Father, belonging to the Son, belonging to one another, the Spirit living in us, all these things start to make sense in John 14:20. Without eyes and ears people are blind and deaf.

Keep my commands

In verse 21 Jesus says a very humbling thing, 'Whoever has my commands and keeps them is the one who loves me.

The one who loves me will be loved by my Father, and I too will love them and show myself to them.' Don't you find it unsettling when Jesus says, 'If you love me you will keep the commandments'? You say to yourself, 'I'm not really keeping the commandments, my love is terrible.' In our best moments we know that our love for Jesus is feeble and cool, we are so grateful for his steadfast, hot love for us. So the question I want to ask is, 'Does Jesus teach that obedience is crucial to our security?' No, the faithfulness of Jesus is our security. He is faithful to us, his love for us makes us secure. Where does our love for him fit in? The Bible's answer is that our love for him increases the intimacy and the enjoyment of that security. A very simple example is when you take your children on holiday. You put them into their little seats, put their seat belts on, shut the doors and you take the wheel. The security of your children is that you're driving, they are in their seats and the doors are closed, that's their security. But those of you who have driven small children on long distances will know that their obedience is a big part of the happiness of the journey and a big part of the happiness of the holiday! I think that's what Jesus is saying here: our obedience has the wonderful effect of increasing the intimacy, not our security.

In verse 22 the other Judas questions why Jesus is going to show himself to so few people: you're the Messiah, why be so private, why be so restrictive, why not show yourself to everybody? And Jesus gives the very profound reply, 'I'm not going to discuss global strategies with you, Judas. If you've got a receptive heart, you'll get this. The person who's drawn towards me, they will really find Father, Son and Holy Spirit.' So I think Jesus is saying here, 'Don't question my plans, Judas, that's a big mistake, rather question your heart. Is it receptive? Is it open? Is it soft? Is it humble? We will make our home in such a heart.' This word 'home' in verse 23 is only used here and in John 14:2 where Jesus says, 'My Father's house has many rooms.' So to put all this together, Jesus is simply saying, 'If you are receptive and give a home to the living God, the living God will be receptive and give you an eternal home.' Christianity is not very complicated is it? Welcome him, he'll welcome you. Refuse him, he'll refuse you.

Our teacher

Now the second tutorial: in verses 25–31 we learn the Spirit is our teacher. Verse 25, 'All this I've spoken while still with you,' is directed primarily to the apostles. Friends, do beware of seeing yourself in every verse. I know it's exciting; it's like looking at photos, isn't it? 'There I am! There I am!' A lot of John 14 – 16 is exclusively for the apostles and when we realize this it will hugely help our Christian life. So in verse 26 the Holy Spirit is going to teach the apostles. Let's not be in any confusion about this – the Holy Spirit is going to come and in the next weeks, months and years, teach those apostles and remind them of everything Jesus said. This doesn't mean the Holy Spirit is going to teach the eleven disciples all the topics of the world but he's going to teach them all the things they need to be men of faith and faithfulness. And John 14:26 goes a long way to explaining how these very slow disciples remembered the very long speeches of Jesus. How does John remember what Jesus said in chapter 5, 6, 7, 8, 9, 10, 11, 12, 13, 14, 15, 16, 17? The Holy Spirit will enable, teach and remind. And Peter explained that the Holy Spirit drove the apostles on like little sailing boats enabling them to record the Scriptures (2 Peter 1:21).

I want to also say to you, friends, don't be ashamed of your Bibles. It's increasingly difficult, isn't it, to be proud of our Bibles? In the post-modern world we often hide our Bibles away. But Jesus said, 'If anyone is ashamed of me and my words, I'll be ashamed of him.' Don't be ashamed of your Bible. The Bible is a miraculous book. It's something we should not only be very grateful for but also very proud of how God has put it together. And whatever technology comes along words are still going to be the most precise communication we have. Of course, the Holy Spirit is going to teach every generation but we are not like the apostles being taught in order that we might record the Scriptures. We are going to be taught what is recorded in the Scriptures in order that we would appreciate them. So please remember things that you hear and are preached to you and ask for the help of the Holy Spirit to drive them home. Remember John Stott's famous prayer that he prayed again and again before he preached, 'Lord Jesus, we bow in your presence. May your Word be our rule and guide.' Remember the next sentence? 'Your Holy Spirit our teacher, your great glory our supreme concern.'

Well, with God's Word in our hearts it's no accident that peace follows (verse 27). Truth, peace – peace, truth, they go together. Peace and truth are related; read what Jesus achieved on the cross, read the promises which apply to you, and know the peace. Jesus does his atoning work, he provides short promises and he gives his peace to us.

And, finally, in verse 28 Jesus says to the apostles they should be glad that, 'I am going to the Father, for the Father is greater than I.' This is a very dangerous text in the wrong hands, especially in the hands of cults. The cults say, 'There you are: Jesus is inferior, the Father is greater.' But read the context. The Father is in heaven, Jesus is on the earth; the Father is in splendour, Jesus is in trouble; the Father is in perfection and Jesus is going to judgment. Where would you rather be? Jesus belongs in heaven, no wonder he is keen to return. He longs to return where he belongs, where the Father is, in a greater position and a greater place. Verse 30 tells us the devil is coming to do what God has decided he will do because he's a dog on a leash.

Change happens

And look at verse 31, why does Jesus go to the cross? Well, he goes to the cross because he loves you (John 3:16). But primarily he goes to the cross because he loves the Father. His obedience and his love for the Father are all caught up in this absolutely perfect faithfulness to his Father. When we read these verses together we realize that Jesus has done his work of going and the Holy Spirit has come and has indwelt the believer forever. The Spirit will teach us the things that are in the Scriptures if we put away rubbishy things and ask him to help; we are sluggish and slow but the Holy Spirit will feed us with the Scriptures in a way that nothing in the world could ever do. When we realize all of this we understand a little bit of the privilege of this gift of the Holy Spirit, changing us, making us into new people.

Notes

1. Graham Cole, *Engaging with the Holy Spirit* (Inter-Varsity Press, 2007).

3. Fruit That Lasts: John 15:1–27

Here in John 15 we see Jesus teaching the disciples that through the Holy Spirit's power they are going to bear fruit that lasts. The immeasurable privilege of being a Christian is to bear fruit that lasts, and whatever we are doing in the short term we need to have that eternal perspective. You remember the psalmist said, 'Lord, you are eternal, you are forever, you are endless, we are so temporary, we are so fleeting, we are like the mist, please could you establish the work of our hands' (Psalm 90, author's translation). And Jesus says, 'You'll bear fruit that lasts.' Or the writer of Ecclesiastes, the great pessimist thinking of the world under the hot sun says, 'Nothing really matters, nothing really lasts, everything disappears, it's a kind of waste of time,' and Jesus says, 'You'll bear fruit that lasts.' And there are millions of earthly prizes which are going to look very stupid in eternity. But the person that you've prayed for, written to, invited, loved, spoken the gospel to, sent something to read or listen to, is going to be under God's good hand effected for eternity. God is at work through his people doing eternal good.

Now in case John 15 is just too familiar I want to remind you how helpful this passage is for living the Christian life. Is it not a wonderful thing to be able to get up in the morning and think, 'I've just so many things to think about, I've got so many issues'? And Jesus says in John 15 to remain in him, love the believers, be a witness to the lost. The sequence, the order, the beauty of John 15 is one of the great gifts to us. And I hope that in those times when your Christian life does seem to be overwhelmed, when there are too many things to think about and too many issues to cope with, you might just go back to John 15 and say, 'Lord, this is what you've asked me to do: walk with you, love your people, be a witness. I can't do everything, there's a lot of things I can't do, please help me to do these three.'

Remaining in Christ – verses 1–8

Jesus says in John 15:1, 'I am the true vine, and my Father is the gardener.' This is the seventh of the 'I am' statements in the book of John and it's a very brilliant illustration to introduce vine and branches. Jesus has been teaching about the Holy Spirit and new life in his people, about the intimacy of relationships, belonging to the Father, belonging to the Son, belonging to the Spirit, God in them, the Spirit of Christ in them, the Holy Spirit in them – all these intimate relationships. How appropriate then to talk about vine and branches.

Those who knew their Old Testament would know that the Old Testament is full of *vine* teaching. 'You brought a vine out of Egypt, you drove out the nations and planted it,' but 'your vine is cut down . . . restore us, O Lord' (Psalm 80). Isaiah 5:2 says the Lord had a vineyard and 'planted it with the choicest vines [Israel]. Then he looked for a crop of good grapes but it yielded only bad fruit.'

And Jesus sits round the table with the disciples and he says to them that the Old Testament disciples failed to produce the fruit. He doesn't say, 'You New Testament disciples will produce the good fruit.' He says, 'I'm the vine, you're the branches.' He'll produce the fruit through us. The Old Testament believers failed, we New Testament believers would fail but he will not fail. He will bear the fruit that he is looking for.

So if Jesus is the vine, the Father is the gardener, believers are the branches and the purpose is fruit. This may explain why God cuts and prunes, which sounds very difficult, and why some of us have been experiencing hardships which have brought about good things. The fruit that God is looking for is lasting fruit, and that outweighs the short-term costs.

What is the fruit? Did you pick it up as John 15 was read for us, because it's not actually defined in the chapter? There is no point or verse where Jesus actually says, 'Now

I am going to tell you what the fruit is.' But we can guess that the fruit has to do with remaining in Christ, loving the believers and testifying to the lost. In other words we can assume that the answer is in the chapter. Now verse 8 provides some help in this. It says, 'This is to my Father's glory, that you bear much fruit.' Verse 16 gives us another clue to the fruit – it's what God desires: 'I . . . appointed you so that you might go and bear fruit.' So we can be pretty sure that the fruit is something which brings God glory, it's what he desires and that is fellowship with Christ, loving one another and, if possible, being used by God to help people come to Christ.

Now the big emphasis in verses 1–8 is to *remain in Christ*. The word 'remain' actually comes ten times in these verses. And it's his grace, of course, which has grafted us into him, but we have a responsibility to stick close, and the reason that he calls us to do this is because he's not interested in professional Christianity. I'm getting old, some of you are getting old and it is a great danger for us in the Christian life to get stale. We've heard it all, we've said it all and we've sung it all. And what we're really spouting is old clichés; nobody can fault them but they are quite sleepy and tired. And I want to say to you on the basis of the whole Bible, but especially John 15, Jesus is not interested in that kind of distant, old, cold, professional relationship. He is too jealous a husband for that. He is not satisfied with a cold marriage. He does not want you to walk round with a text book in your hand and that's it, or turn up at conventions and hear talks and that's it.

He is a person, you're a person and he is interested in close, warm, intimate fellowship with you. The cross has removed the barriers to make that possible and the Holy Spirit has brought new life into your heart to make that something you should long for. And Jesus calls on us to remain, to abide, and to stick close. Now surely that's why John 15:7 says, 'If you remain in me and my words remain in you, ask whatever you wish, and it will be done for you.' Do you notice what's there in verse 7? Scripture and prayer. You may think that it's only dull preachers who finish every sermon by saying, 'Read your Bible and say your prayers', but the greatest teacher of all saw this as the key to good fellowship. Take in the words, lift up your prayers.

Somebody has said that almost 90% of sermons finish with the application, 'Read your Bible, say your prayers, go to church and witness to the unbeliever.' There is something tedious about that, isn't there? And yet there is something that's utterly necessary about it. So we must fight the idea that these things will ever be stale. Verse 7a: 'If . . . my words remain,' verse 7b: 'ask whatever you wish.' Friends, ask God to save you from unhappy Bible reading and unhappy praying. Send up your little prayer; say to him, 'I'm going to read the Bible, please help me. I'm a very deaf and dull person, please help me. I'm going to pray, please help me because I give up very quickly.'

These are the keys to our fellowship with the Lord Jesus and every real Christian knows the difference between the dry orthodoxy which just turns the wheels, plays the game, goes to Keswick, and the fresh fellowship which Jesus seeks and gives. We need to ask him for it, we need to read the Bible for it and we need to pray for it. And I don't know any shortcut to good fellowship with Jesus other than being a humble listener to his Word and being somebody who sends up, even briefly, genuine prayers.

Now because we're complicated people and this remaining is important, the Lord gives us a good mix of promise and warning. We need incentives and we need alarm bells and you will find plenty of incentives and alarm bells in verses 1–8. The incentive is Jesus' desire to bear much fruit through you. The warning is that the fruitless branch goes to the fire. We need the promise and the warning in the Christian life. Our fears need the promises; our sins need the warnings. I know we would like to reduce the whole of Christianity to a slogan or a bumper sticker, but God is too clever, too wise; he's too brilliant a pastor for that. So we need John 10:28: 'No one will snatch them out of my hand,' and we need John 15:2: if you are fruitless you may go to the fire. We need them both, not because they contradict each other – they don't contradict each other – but because God is the perfect pastor and he knows we are capable of lurching from fear to foolishness. He gives us the promises and the warnings so that we'll be safe.

Now verse 2 is a very frightening text: 'He cuts off every branch in me that bears no fruit.' It certainly would have applied to Judas who had just left the room; the others were clean and Jesus had great hopes for them. This verse is not meant to unsettle or preoccupy you, but it is meant to be a caution so that you will say, 'I don't want to be a fruitless branch.' If you find yourself utterly in despair, go to John 10:28: no one will ever pluck you out of Christ's hand. But if you are in that casual position where nothing really matters and you don't care, and you think you are getting the best of sin and salvation it might be not a bad thing to go to John 15:2 and ask yourself whether this is a fruitful time. As long as you don't let this verse 2 preoccupy you, it's a good warning.

What we are to concentrate on is close fellowship with Christ. Maybe you need to finish this morning by bowing your head and praying for a few seconds that God would help you to have a real walk with him, that what has got too distant, too separate and too stale would be refreshed and renewed. Even when we find ourselves being pruned – which by definition is hurtful, painful and costly – the person who is doing this is the Father who loves you. None of it is being done with any sadistic carelessness; it's being done with great, great affection, love and purpose.

Here is Jesus about to leave, and his top priority for the disciples is that they will walk with him. How badly things go when we substitute other people for Christ, work for Christ or family for Christ. There is no fruit when we are distant. So take up the privilege of being a branch in the vine which you are if your faith is in Christ. Rejoice that his Spirit is in you; there is no barrier because he died for you. Take in his words, lift up your prayers and there will be fruit to his glory. And when God says, 'This is to my . . . glory' (verse 8), he doesn't mean *ego*. We give God glory not because he has a big ego. Ego is disproportionate to what is deserved. When we give glory to God we are just beginning to glimpse a little bit of what he deserves. The best praise we ever offer at Keswick doesn't come close to what we will one day offer him when we see him face to face. And he knows, of course, when we give him glory and our hearts rise up to him, that's good for us because we are coming home to the harbour where our hearts belong. So 'remain,' says Jesus. It's to his glory; it's to the Father's glory.

Loving the brethren – verses 9–17

Jesus refers to the churches in verses 12 and 17 as being great instruments in God's hand to help people wake up and take notice of him. Christians are to love one another, and Jesus explains this will be one of the big reasons people will know we are his. There are huge numbers of people who have become Christians because of the loving fellowship of God's people. God is at work through the local church, and Jesus says to keep loving one another because this is a very powerful instrument for fruit that lasts. I often tell my congregation in North Sydney, 'You won't find love and truth at the football, you won't find love and truth at a big blockbuster movie, you won't find love and truth at the circus, you won't find love and truth at a party, but you'll find love and truth in the little local church, and they outweigh a whole lot of things that are going on at movies, football games and parties.' And as the world becomes more and more dishonest, and it is becoming more and more dishonest, and as the world becomes more and more selfish, and it is, the local church is going to be a brighter and brighter light in a dark world, so keep working at your love for one another.

How are we going to get interested in loving one another? Well, we get some clues in John 15. First of all in verse 9: know where you stand yourself. Is verse 9 not one of the most remarkable verses in the whole Bible? 'As the Father has loved *me* so have I loved *you*.' And you say, 'That's impossible; the Father loves you and you deserve it but you couldn't love me like that.' And Jesus says, 'Yes, the Father has loved me perfectly and eternally, and I love you, perfectly and eternally; that's the fact. You are a greatly loved person.' And I want you to notice how often in the New Testament Jesus uses the word 'loved' rather than just 'loves'. 'Loved' is highly significant. Jesus doesn't mean, 'I've loved you in the past and I don't love you now in the present.' He means, 'I've loved you in the past and that's how I love you in the present. It's a steadfast, fixed, flag in the ground; I've *loved* you, it's established, it's decided, I've *loved* you.'

That's why Paul says in Romans 8:37, 'We're more than conquerors through him who *loved* us.' Galatians 2:20: 'I no longer live, but Christ lives in me. The life I now live . . . I live by faith in the Son of God who *loved* me.' 1 John 4:10, 'This is love: not that we loved God but that he *loved* us.' Again and again, it's in the past tense. So fix it in your mind that he *loved* you. Think Calvary and, therefore, he loves you. And therefore, friends, you can go out on a limb and speak to someone about Jesus because you are not dependent on the response you get from that person for your security. You can cross a floor as a loved person and not get very much back from the conversation, but you're absolutely fine. You're loved at the start of the walk and at the finish of the walk, whatever took place. Some of God's people are difficult; they are not as sweet as me! But regardless, we are much loved, remind yourself!

Secondly, obedience blesses the relationship. John 15:10: 'If you keep my commands, you will remain in my love, just as I've kept my Father's commands and remain in his love.' Now he's not saying that your security will hang on your obedience. What he's saying is your intimacy with him and others will be greatly affected by your obedience. It's not that your failure to obey will remove you; it is that your obedience will bless you and so Jesus commands this love. Verse 10: it's not an option, he's the Teacher, he's the Lord. We must do the loving and he calls us his friends. Incidentally, in the New Testament we don't get to call Jesus 'friend'. He is the Friend of sinners but you don't find in the New Testament that he's being addressed as friend. It's a new challenge, I think, for those who work with children who want to say, 'Jesus is your friend.' It's not a bad thing to say; it's not necessarily a wrong thing to say; it's just not a great New Testament priority. And perhaps we would elevate the Lord Jesus in the minds of many young people if we reminded them that Jesus is our Shepherd, our King, our Master and our Saviour. We call him Teacher and Lord; he calls us his friends.

And when we obey him and we love his people, he uses this for great good in the world. Sometimes when Kathy and I are walking to a dinner that we know is not going to be particularly easy, we pray as we walk, 'Lord, we're not very good at this, we're feeling quite weary, not particularly loving. Would you please help us, would you please enable us, would you please use us?' Imagine walking into a gathering which is full of people who've said, 'How can I be helpful to someone else?' It's going to mark itself in the world, isn't it? It's going to be a very different community from what the world is experiencing.

Thirdly, realize what love means. In verse 12 Jesus says, 'My command is this: Love each other as I have loved you.' He explains, 'I'm not asking you to love people as you feel love should be felt; I'm not asking you to love people as the world loves people; I'm asking you to love people as I've loved you.' This, of course, doesn't mean that we are going to lay down our life and die for them. We're certainly not going to save them, but we may put away self-interest; we may tip out the last drop of what we have for someone else and discover that God wonderfully fills the cup and enables us to be replenished, even as we thought we were at the end of our resources.

The battle – verses 15–18

In verse 18 we come to the hatred and the opposition. It's quite a contrast to the love of verse 17. 'If the world hates you, keep in mind that it hated me first.' No wonder it's easier to hang round Christian circles! '*If* the world hates you,' basically means, *when* the world hates you. This is not the round world, this is not the green hills of Keswick, this is not the geography, this is the cosmos, this is the rebellious world, this is the hostile world, this is the world, the system, that says we rotate on ourselves. And if you echo self, and some churches are starting to do that, you are largely left alone by the world. Because the church that is just echoing, 'You're the centre of the universe,' is saying exactly what the world wants to hear. But if you present as clearly as you can that there is someone who is truly and genuinely at the centre of the universe and his name is Jesus Christ, you'll feel the hostility. It is the most important message in the universe, it honours Jesus, it saves people, it's true to you, but it's not what the world wants to hear. It's what the world needs to hear.

John Piper says very helpfully that we in the West are not in the fires of persecution but we are in the freezer. I think he's exactly right. We're not going to get burnt at the stake but we will feel the cold hostility to the gospel. Don't be surprised, keep going. When I used to visit houses in North Sydney, I would knock on doors and be my normal charming self. People would say, 'Thanks very much, you're a slightly annoying person, thanks for the leaflet, please leave as fast as you can.' That was the gist of it. It's all changed in the last twenty years. Now if I go visiting the attitude is: 'This is just inappropriate, you shouldn't be here, this is wrong, I don't care who you are, you shouldn't be here.' It's a hostile, cold freeze. And Jesus wants to equip the apostles and us to cope with this, so he says they are not the first to be opposed, keep in mind it hated him first. Jesus was the lightning rod for three years; the church is the lightning rod, but we are actually suffering *for him*. He is the one who is hated; don't be surprised, says Jesus in verse 18; don't expect to feel at home (verse 19). If you belong to the world it would love you as its own, but you've been chosen out of the world so you are something of an alien. Do you not feel a little bit of an alien? Do you not feel the difficulty of living in a Christ-centred universe when the world that you're in doesn't see, care, acknowledge, act or respond? You're an alien! You've been chosen out of the world. Verse 20: 'Remember what I told you: "A servant is not greater than his master." If they persecuted me, they will persecute you also.' Jesus lived his life perfectly, beautifully, wonderfully, and he was hated. And so you may live your life in a godly way and the strange, but not so strange thing, is that you'll be hated.

Verse 21: the world is blind, the world is ignorant. But they are still guilty because Jesus has come and they have no excuse for their sin (verse 22). There is the combination. Those lovely people who live near us and who in some ways are nicer than we are but don't acknowledge Jesus, are heading for hell. They are blind but they are responsible; we need to keep those two in mind as we pray for them. And then verse 23: the world is doing what God said the world would do all along; it's just fulfilling the script. Verse 25: 'This is to fulfil what is written in their law: "They hated me without reason."' God is not taken by surprise;

we are not to be taken by surprise. Don't think to yourself when you act faithfully and people respond dreadfully, 'I could have done that better.' Maybe you could have or maybe if somebody else had said it, it would have been successful and effective. But it may not be that way at all; it may be that all these verses of John 15 are coming true.

Now if you jump from 15:25 to 16:2, you see that we move from secular opposition to religious opposition because Jesus says, 'They will put you out of the synagogue; in fact, the time is coming when anyone who kills you will think they are offering a service to God.' We move from secular opposition to religious opposition, and I don't need to remind you that religious opposition can be worse. Jesus says religious opposition may mean that people are killing others, thinking they are serving their God. But they are doing this because they are ignorant of God (verse 3). There's a politically incorrect sentence for you. People of other religions don't know God because you can only know God through Jesus. 'I am the way and the truth and the life. No one comes to the Father except by me' (John 14:6).

You notice that between the secular opposition of chapter 15 and the religious opposition of chapter 16 comes the third little seminar on the Holy Spirit. The Holy Spirit (15:26–27) 'whom I will send to you from the Father . . . he will testify about me. And you also must testify'. Jesus says, 'This Holy Spirit who is in you forever and will teach you is going to testify; that is his great delight. And you will testify because you've been with me from the beginning.' Now, of course, we haven't been with Jesus from the beginning like the apostles, but we're going to testify as part of the relay team and he will be with us. 'And surely I am with you always, to the very end of the age' (Matthew 28:20). But the wonder, beauty and genius of the Holy Spirit in this particular little seminar is that he is testifying to the world about Jesus and he is in charge of the case for Christ. He orchestrates it around the world, he supervises it, he is successful, he knows what he's doing, he's not stuck, he's not shocked, he's not thrown backwards, he knows exactly what he's doing. Imagine if it was up to the local bishops? Imagine if it was all up to the mission organizations? The Holy Spirit is in charge of the testifying and he will use us in the case. He uses us in the way we live and the way we speak. Sometimes we initiate a conversation, we proclaim Christ (Colossians 1) and sometimes we answer somebody (Colossians 4).

One of the secrets, I think, for many of you who go back to normal lives this coming week is that you are not asked to go to work, get on a soapbox and preach a sermon. What you are asked to do in the words of Colossians 4 is 'live wisely'. So when a conversation opens, 'What did you do last week?' You say, 'Well, believe it or not I went to a large gathering of keen Christian people.' That's all you say. 'Really? I thought you were intelligent?' 'I'm reasonably intelligent but a lot of people there were more intelligent than me.' That's all you say. 'And what did you do at the Convention?' 'Well, we listened to a guy from a long way away and he opened the Bible.' 'Really? I thought the Bible was a dead, boring book?' And on you go just answering their questions. One of the great joys of the Christian life is to be an answerer.

Here in this very complex and difficult world in which we live with secular and religious opposition the Holy Spirit is organizing a mission. He has come and taken up residence in your life. He will help you to walk with Jesus, love one another, and testify, in order that you might bear fruit that lasts.

4. Advantage Believer: John 16:1–33

Do you remember the argument so far? Jesus will leave, the Spirit will come and we are to work on three relationships which are crucial – walk with Jesus, love the believers and be a witness to the lost. Now the section today, verses 5–33, is the most complex and it introduces the fourth and the fifth seminar on the Holy Spirit. Remember seminar one in chapter 14 – the Holy Spirit will indwell you forever; seminar two – he will remind and teach; seminar three – he'll testify to Christ: he works on the case for Christ in the world and he'll use the believers in the case. And today we come to the fourth seminar in chapter 16 – he is going to expose the world, expose unbelievers; and the fifth seminar – he's going to glorify Jesus. There is a beautiful sweep in these five seminars, don't miss them: he'll indwell you, he'll teach you, he'll use you as a witness, he'll work in the world, he'll give the glory to Jesus.

So let's look at the first of these sections. The first section is going to be by far the longest. We are going to spend three quarters of our time on the first ten verses and a quarter of our time on the last verses. That is not to short change the last verses but I think the argument demands that we give more time to the beginning. So look at John 16:5, 'Now I am going to him who sent me yet none of you asks me, "Where are you going?"' Isn't that an odd thing to say? Did not Peter say in chapter 13, 'Lord, where are you going?' Did not Thomas say in chapter 14:5, 'Lord, we don't know where you are going'? Yet Jesus says that none of them asks him where he is going. I want to challenge you as you read your Bible not to skim over these things but to ask the hard questions: why does he say this?

Preoccupied believers

I mentioned on Monday the disciples have only been concerned that Jesus is leaving; nobody has really cared where he's going. Just as you might say to somebody who walks out of this auditorium, 'Where are you going?' You're not interested in where they're going, you're concerned that they're leaving. And these disciples that have been with Jesus for three years are utterly self-preoccupied. They're not interested in him, they're not interested in his mission, they are very interested in themselves. Now, friends, we get frustrated by people who are just interested in themselves and people get very frustrated with us because we are just interested in ourselves. But what is it like for Jesus to have a body of believers like us who are just self-excited and self-preoccupied? He's amazing to put up with us, isn't he? Just imagine having to listen to everybody's prayers, eighty-five million requests for a parking spot every second! Unbelievable!

That's the small issue: Jesus is leaving but they don't really care. The big issue is when Jesus says, 'It's for your good that I am going away. Unless I go the Advocate will not come; but if I go I will send him' (verse 7). Jesus needs to die and rise so there can be intimate fellowship between God and us, and the Spirit is the proof or the seal of that intimacy. And Jesus explains that when the Spirit comes there will be an advantage. Now we can think of lots of advantages for the coming of the Holy Spirit – he causes us to come to life, he causes us to understand the Scriptures, he helps us in our prayers, he causes fruit to be borne, and he even gives us access so we are able to go back to our room or sit under a tree and have the most intimate and accessible fellowship with God. Because Jesus has died and the Spirit has come you are able to come to the very throne of grace. But the advantage that Jesus actually wants to discuss is in verse 8. He wants to talk about the advantage of the Spirit coming to convict the world of sin, righteousness and judgment.

Working in partnership with the Spirit

Now do you expect the Holy Spirit to march out alone into

the world convicting people while we sit at home? Do we expect the Holy Spirit to travel the streets causing people who are sitting in their houses, maybe in foreign lands, to suddenly fall under conviction? Or should we hold onto the last verses of chapter 15 where Jesus said, 'He will testify . . . you also must testify'? In other words, it will be through you that the Spirit will do his work. Do you expect the Holy Spirit to go out and strike down the nations? Or do you expect him to do that as the Word, which is his sword, is distributed, preached, shared and proclaimed (Ephesians 6)? Do you see the issue I am trying to ask you? Do you think the Holy Spirit will do this independently or is he going to do this in partnership? Do we want to separate Spirit and believers in the work of evangelism? Do we want to separate Spirit and Word in the work of evangelism?

Now I think the theological answer to this is that we shouldn't limit what the Spirit may do. But the normal working of the Spirit is with his sword, the Word, in the hands of his people. Historically that is the way the Spirit has worked. We shouldn't limit, of course, how people may believe or how they may come under conviction. God is sovereign and he is able to bring people under conviction through all sorts of ways. Praise God! And yet the normal work of God is to bring people under conviction through the gospel.

Romans 10:13 is very important, isn't it? 'Everyone who calls on the name of the Lord will be saved,' says Paul. Then, 'How are they going to call unless someone preaches to them?' He doesn't fall for the argument in Romans 1: there's a creation, that'll do it. He doesn't fall for Romans 2: there's a conscience, that'll do it. No, says Paul, there is a creation, there is a conscience, Christ has come, and someone needs to tell them. The Spirit works with his people, with the Word, normally, primarily, usually, wonderfully. And this is not just an academic exercise for us this morning, because if you decide that nobody can believe unless we and the missionary agencies are involved, we may actually miss much of what God is doing in the world. But if we decide that we are not needed and we can sit in Keswick and God will do it without us, we are going to cut the cord of mission and urgency and we're in danger of ignoring Jesus' charge, 'You . . . must testify.' I hope that dilemma makes sense.

The convicting work of the Spirit is talked about in these verses, and it does not follow that just because the Spirit will do the convicting work he's on his own. The convicting work of the Spirit in somebody may be done in sovereign isolation but the text doesn't say that, and we know from the rest of Scripture that God is pleased to use servants with the Word in their hands, that's the normal way. The mission that we are called to involves Christian people with the gospel. So I want to say, don't separate what God joins. Don't sit and think, 'Well, someone else will do it,' or 'God will do it without me,' when God invites us in his great love and power to be his partners in the work. We must join together the convicting work of the Spirit, without which nobody would believe, the very

Word of God, and the opportunities we've been given. Let's join it all together, because that's the way the Bible talks.

Guilty as charged

Now when the Spirit convicts the world, and imagine that is hand in hand with a Christian sharing the gospel, Jesus doesn't mean that the Spirit is going to convince God that people are guilty. Jesus is not saying the Spirit is going to win a court case in heaven so that God will suddenly say, 'You're right, they're sinful.' The world stands guilty, we know that from John 3. Jesus the Light has come into the world, men love darkness, the world stands guilty. Because of Jesus the wrath of God sits like a sword above every unbeliever. Now the Spirit is going to bring conviction home to the unbeliever, that's the wonderful thing. The Spirit is going to cause the non-Christian to see where he or she stands with God. I want to summarize this in two sentences. The first is the world stands guilty because Jesus has come. The second is the world learns its guilt because the Spirit convicts.

I'm so thankful that God brought conviction to me in my last year of school. I remember sitting in a co-ed camp; I'd gone because it was co-ed! I sat in the very back row, I wasn't interested; how kind of God to bring me under great conviction of my sin. I realized that I was a sneaky, sinful boy and I went up to the guy at the end and said, 'What can I do?' And he had the wit to say, 'You can't do anything,' and he explained the gospel. I'm so grateful to God that he brought me to see the bad news and the good news. I bumped into a friend yesterday who became a Christian in his late seventies. He's humble about his sin, grateful for Jesus and it's just wonderful to see. One of the men in our congregation, a big burly Greek builder, was converted when he read Acts 9:4, 'Why do you persecute me?' He burst into tears under conviction. What a wonderful thing: the Word of God in the hand of the Spirit bringing conviction.

Now this is how Jesus describes the conviction in verse 9: he will bring conviction 'of sin because people don't believe in me'. Look at that, that's a good definition of sin, not believing in Jesus. And we realize, therefore, that the fundamental problem is not random lies we told, random lusts we felt, but that we're centrally wrong about Jesus. And so the Spirit clears the fog and we suddenly say, 'It's all about him.' Verse 10: he brings conviction of righteousness; he shames the person to realize that the righteousness of Christ is massive and the righteousness that we have is desperately dreadful and embarrassing.

No longer do we have a low view of Jesus and a high view of self, we now have a high view of Jesus and a low view of self, and everything has been turned right way up. He convicts people of righteousness and then, verse 11, he brings conviction of judgment. Partly this is recognizing the judging work of Jesus winning victoriously at the cross. But partly it's the healthy fear of judgment. No longer do we talk about judgment as though it was a joke, and laugh that if we do end up in hell all the fun people will be there. What a terrible lie that is. The Holy Spirit brings a healthy fear to us and we run to Christ.

Now, friends, do you see what Jesus is saying? The Holy Spirit convicts people of righteousness and judgment because they are hearing the gospel, they are hearing about Jesus, they are hearing about his righteousness which they lack, they are hearing about judgment and their need. That's how the Holy Spirit does his convicting work. And if none of that means much to you, if you are the sort of person who thinks everything I'm saying today is just background noise, maybe you haven't heard it, maybe you've never got it, maybe you're blind.

I worked with a very fine minister for a few years – many of you will know him – Dick Lucas, in London. And I went to a cocktail party and I was cornered by a huge Englishman who prodded me in the chest and told me that Christianity was just, 'Do your best.' I didn't know what to say so I said to Dick, 'What do we do at English cocktail parties when someone pins you in a corner and just tells you to, "Do your best"?' He said, 'Well, that's an interesting question. During the week I spoke to Harrow School and the Lord blessed the talk. I went back to the common room with all the staff, and the senior science master came over to me and said, "That was an excellent talk, Mr Lucas, very good for the boys. They need that; I'm a scientist so, of course, I can't believe any of that."' Dick said he took a step closer and he put his face right up against this man's face and he said, 'No, the reason you don't believe is because you're blind. And the reason you are blind is that you are a very proud and sinful man and you'll never be able to see until you repent and put your faith in Jesus.' Isn't that a great conversation? Now I'm not asking you to be rude, I'm just asking you occasionally to be brave. People are blind; maybe they need to be told.

I want to summarize now some important things from what I've said. The Spirit drives this conviction home, not in heaven – God doesn't need to be told we're guilty – but the Spirit drives it home in the human heart. The Spirit shames the unbeliever into seeing their view of Jesus is hopeless, their view of righteousness inadequate, their view of judgment plain wrong. We might say that sin has been shown to be deeper than we ever realized, righteousness higher than we ever realized, judgment closer than we ever realized, and so we call to Christ and everything about him becomes clear, and everything about self becomes clear, and we move out of the fog into the light.

The instrument the Holy Spirit uses again and again is the gospel. Romans 1:16: 'For I am not ashamed of the gospel, because it is the power of God that brings salvation.' Do not cut the link between the Spirit working and the servant of God with the gospel. If you cut the link, mission urgency will die, mission usefulness will die, people will die.

God knows what he's doing

Now, friends, why is there so little conviction today? Well, the simple answer is, it depends where you live. Dinesh

D'Souza has written a great book, *What's so great about Christianity?*[1] He says if you think the church is not growing you live in the wrong suburb. The church is growing. Some places have got very few coming under conviction, like Australia, like the UK, but there are places where people are coming under conviction in their thousands. When the work is hard, let me say to you – and I say this to myself – don't fall into the trap of thinking things are too difficult for God. Do not fall into the trap of thinking people are too hard for God; that is just man-centred Christianity. If you are beginning to think that God sits in heaven wringing his hands just wishing desperately that someone would take him seriously, you're in fantasy land. You are not in Bible land.

I always remember Tim Keller saying once he lost all small views of Jesus when he went on a camp. The speaker asked the young people there to imagine they were going to make a model of the galaxy. The scale of the model of the galaxy, the distance between the sun and the earth, is going to be the thickness of a piece of paper. 'Now,' said the speaker, 'how big a room do you need to do the galaxy on that model?' You need a room 700 kilometres by 700 kilometres by 500 kilometres to get the galaxy in as a model, and the speaker said, 'Since Jesus rules and governs billions of galaxies he's not your mascot.' It's a great reminder, isn't it? Jesus is huge. Sometimes I ask myself, how can he even see the speck of dust that we're walking on. Don't fall into the trap of thinking he's stuck, just keep going with the task that you've been given. We know that he delights to see people saved, but it seems to be his decree in parts of the West that people are not coming in great numbers. The man-centred view is to say God is having trouble; the Bible's view is to say that God is utterly sovereign. We must get our RSVP into him, which most of you have done, and then we must get the invitations out as best we can. That's our job. Remember Jesus doing miracles, preaching in the cities, and nobody takes any notice of him, and he says, 'I thank you, heavenly Father, you hide, you reveal, you're totally in charge' (Matthew 11:25, author's translation), and he suddenly turns round and says, 'Come, all you who are weary and burdened and I'll give you rest' (Matthew 11:28), because the gospel goes on like a river: if it hits a rock it moves around it; it climbs a fence like a vine; if it hits a post it climbs over it. Just keep moving with the gospel, don't give up, God knows what he's doing.

The Spirit and the Word

Now the fifth and final tutorial on the Holy Spirit comes in verses 12–14. This is the climax because the Holy Spirit is working all for Christ's glory. John 16:13: 'He will guide you into all truth,' that is, all the truth you need for salvation and service. The Holy Spirit is not an independent thinker, he will convey what he has been given. He's like an executor of a will – he's going to pass on what is there, he's not going to invent stuff, he's not going to keep stuff, he's going to pass on what he's been given. And so

Jesus here in the upper room is commissioning the New Testament, because he says to the apostles in chapter 14:26, 'The Holy Spirit . . . will teach you all things and will remind you of everything I have said to you.' And now he says in chapter 16:13, 'He will guide you into all truth,' and 'tell you what is yet to come.' So he launches the New Testament here from the upper room and Peter says in his letters that they were driven by the Holy Spirit to record the Holy Scriptures (2 Peter 1:21). Therefore, if you are going to be led by the Spirit he's not going to take you away from the Scriptures. If your church thinks it's more exciting to move away from the Bible, your church is mistaken. The Holy Spirit leads into the Word, that's where the exciting treasures and riches are to be found. And he's going to do that, not only because that's where the treasures and riches are to be found, but because he's obedient to his task.

I want to speak as to dear friends and say two things which I think are real confusions in the church at the moment. Two things I need to hear, you need to hear, and maybe they are good for Keswick to hear. Here's the first: I don't know what to do when someone tells me that God will speak to my heart. My heart is corrupt, desperately wicked; if I listen to my heart, I'll probably conclude something quite selfish and sinful. God will speak to me with the Word. I don't mean he can't bring information to me from other directions, but I do want to know that what's been said to me fits the Word. And, therefore, I need to know the Word, where he normally speaks, and if what's being said to me is faithful.

The second thing is, I wonder if it would be a good idea if we stopped saying that we enjoyed talks and sermons. I just can't see the Old Testament prophets having people coming up to them afterwards and saying, 'I enjoyed that.' I can't see people coming down with Jesus from the Sermon on the Mount and saying, 'I got a big kick out of that. That was fun.' Now I don't want to be unfair, I don't want to be rude, I'm just saying to you, would it not be a better idea if we started to think less in consumer terms of enjoying talks and we thought more of valuing talks, appreciating talks? Or maybe you might like to come up to me afterwards and say, 'You know, God was so good to me, I didn't enjoy that at all. That's how good he was.' Well, I'll leave that with you for your thought.

All the work of the Spirit is to glorify Jesus: his work through the Old Testament is to get ready for Jesus; all his work through the New Testament is looking to Jesus. He's wonderful. One of the bishops in Sydney said a passing comment that cut into me deeply. He said, 'I wonder whether the Holy Spirit is interested in what we're doing in proportion to our interest in the glory of Jesus.' What a searching comment! It's exactly what Jesus is saying in 16:14: 'He will glorify me.' When I go to prepare my talk and I find myself saying, 'I hope this goes well,' there's a better prayer: 'Please be glorified.' If I got glorified that would be fun for a minute; if Jesus got glorified it would be right and good.

Now the second point this morning, very briefly, is living in faith and asking in prayer. Verses 16–23 are grappling with one issue and that is, what does Jesus mean when he says, 'In a little while you will see me no more and then after a little while you will see me'? Does he mean, 'I'm leaving at Calvary, I'm back at Easter'? Does he mean, 'I'm leaving at the Ascension; I'll be back at Pentecost by the Spirit'? Does he mean, 'I'll be leaving at the Ascension and I'll be back at the Second Coming'? Well, all three of them involve some grief and joy, don't they? All three of them would fit the gospel. I think we can be pretty sure, however, that Jesus means that he's leaving at Calvary and coming back at the Resurrection. That's his primary meaning because the weeping is appropriate to the weekend more than it is to the fifty days or the two thousand years, and the childbirth illustration is a relatively short struggle, not one that will be drawn out over weeks or years. Verse 22 is a treasure of a text, isn't it? 'Now is your time of grief, but I will see you again and you will rejoice, and no one will take away your joy.' That's what Jesus said to the apostles, and the principle is utterly true for us today, especially when we say farewell to someone we love. The Lord says to us, quite correctly, in the principle of verse 22, 'Now is your time of grief,' you'll see them again, 'and you will rejoice, and no one will take away your joy.' The reunion of 1 Thessalonians 4 is just round the corner.

In Jesus' name

And then, notice in verses 23–28 Jesus says our prayer life is going to be radically different because Jesus goes and the

Spirit comes. The Apostles had been asking Jesus for things for three years; now they are going to ask the Father, and we ask the Father (verse 23). Again, verse 26, their prayers would be in Jesus' name just as we do our praying and ask in Jesus' name. Now we get very used to the phrase, 'in Jesus' name', don't we? I want to say to you this morning that God the Father never gets used to hearing 'in Jesus' name'. It never bores him, never gets predictable, and it never gets stale. When we say, 'in Jesus' name', it hardly means anything to us; when the Father hears, 'in Jesus' name', everything gets moving. Just as if you were a waiter at some special function and, lo and behold, the Prime Minister came over and tapped you on the shoulder and said, 'Could I have some butter?' You go off to the kitchen and you're nobody in the kitchen, but you say, 'The Prime Minister has asked for butter,' everything starts moving, doesn't it? And when you say your prayers, 'in Jesus' name', that's a loaded phrase. It may not mean much to you, but it means everything to the Father. He has made sure that name carries huge significance; all the strength, all the wisdom, lies with him.

The disciples are very feeble. You see, in verse 29 what impresses them is not that Jesus is the supreme Lord and Saviour, but that he knows what people are thinking. Feeble bunch, aren't they? I work with a feeble bunch. Thankfully, they have an absolutely sensational pastor, until he looks in the mirror and sees an utterly feeble pastor, so grateful to his congregation for their prayers, love and support. But we're all feeble, aren't we? All the strength is with the Lord, and Jesus brings them back to earth and says, 'No, you'll desert me but I'm not alone' (verse 32, author's translation). John 16:33: 'In this world you will have trouble. But take heart! I have overcome the world.' Jesus is not a crazy optimist. Listen to Victor Hugo in *The Future of Man*, pre-World War One, 'In the twentieth century war will be dead, hatred will be dead . . . man will live. He will possess something higher than all these – a great country, the whole earth, and a great hope, the whole heaven.' Well, there's a false prophet for you! After World War Two the gloomy pessimist George Orwell imagined the future to be like a boot stamping on a human face forever. There's a false prophet! But here's a true prophet, the true prophet, saying, 'In this world you will have trouble. But take heart! I have overcome the world.'

Notes

1. Dinesh D'Souza, *What's So Great about Christianity?* (Illinois: Tyndale House, 2008).

5. The Real Lord's Prayer: John 17:1–26

The great Spurgeon tells a lovely story of a man walking through a field on one occasion. He bumped into the visiting evangelist who said to him, 'Will you be coming to the tent meetings?' And the man replied, 'No I won't.' Spurgeon said, 'Do you normally go to a church?' And he said, 'No, I never do.' The evangelist said, 'Do you ever pray?' He said, 'I never pray.' The evangelist said, 'I wonder if you would be willing to promise me that if I give you a shilling (which I guess now would be £50), you would never pray again?' The man said, 'I never pray, I'd be happy to do that.' He took the shilling and off he went. Over the next day or two he began to be a little distressed about what he had done. He was haunted by the idea of handing over his prayer life. He thought about the fact that if he was sick, he would not be able to pray; if his children were needy, he'd not be able to intercede. His wife noticed that he was preoccupied and distressed, so she asked him what the matter was and he told her what he'd done. She said, 'You need to hurry to the meeting, find that man and take the whole deal back.' So he hurried off to the tent and found himself in the last meeting with the preacher on the platform speaking on, 'What will it profit a man to gain the whole world and lose his soul?' What will it profit a man to gain the whole world, a shilling, and lose his prayer life? And, of course, he called the evangelist afterwards and begged him to take the deal back, which he was glad to do. And I say this to you because we cannot measure the true value of our prayer life. It is a gift to us.

And today we are turning to the masterful prayer of John chapter 17. This chapter of John is in need of our attention because I suspect that apart from a verse or two most people can't remember what's in this chapter. Jesus is modelling intercession for us and this is the real Lord's prayer, so why don't we know what he prayed? The answer, I think, is we tend to skim read the chapter and it becomes like so much of John, just a bit of a blur. Now we need all the help we can get in our prayers. We know that our prayer life is never going to be free from doubt, guilt, tiredness, struggle, preoccupation and all sorts of things like that. Friends, there is never going to be a book on the bookstall that will make your prayer life a piece of cake; it's just not going to come. You're never going to find a DVD that tells you how to have an easy prayer life. You are never going to go to a conference that will suddenly turn the switch and you'll be praying like a genius. It's just not going to happen. Prayer is part of the spiritual battle (Ephesians 6). Speaking to the invisible God, though we have access, though we are intimate (thanks to the Lord Jesus), though the Holy Spirit helps us, is difficult. It's not an easy two-way conversation; it's a challenging thing. That's why the Lord's prayer is such a gift to us because it's a skeleton on which we can hang so much wisdom and so much intercession.

But having said that it's difficult, there is nothing that is as crucial to us as our prayer life. There's nothing as pure as praying; it's simple fellowship with the Lord Jesus. There's nothing that we do in our Christian life that puts more joy and hope into our walk with Christ. Everything is a struggle when we don't pray. We find out what is important to people when we listen to their prayers, and we are going to find out what is important to Jesus as we look at his prayer.

Now the supper is over, the teaching is over, Jesus lifts up his face towards heaven and he prays. His prayer divides into three parts. In verses 1–5 he prays for himself, in verses 6–19 for the apostles, and then in verses 20–26 for all believers, including us who gather today.

Jesus' prayer for himself

So first of all, let's look at Jesus' prayer for himself. Chapter 17:1: 'Father, the hour has come. Glorify your Son, that your Son may glorify you.' Literally the *time* has come. You remember this time, this hour, has been long coming. The wedding at Cana: the hour has not yet come; John 7 with the brothers: the hour has not yet come; in John 12 the Greeks arrive: the hour has come. And now in John 17 it's really come! The hour of the cross, the glorification followed by resurrection and ascension, this great hour, the work that Jesus has come for, has come. And so Jesus prays. You might say to yourself, 'Why would Jesus pray? It's all organized. God is sovereign, he's loving, he's wise, he's powerful, why pray?' It never occurs to Jesus not to pray. He knows that the Father is sovereign, powerful, loving and wise and, therefore, he is the best person to speak to, and so he does.

He prays for himself first to be glorified. That, I think, should shock us slightly; it should make us sit up and take notice. The Old Testament says that God does not share his glory with another but Jesus unashamedly asks to be glorified, and there are two reasons for this. The first reason is that if Jesus is glorified the Father will be glorified: 'Glorify your Son that your Son may glorify you' (verse 1). The other reason Jesus asks to be glorified is that this will bring people eternal life (verse 2). If Jesus is glorified through his work on the cross, people will have the great invitation to eternal life. That's why he says that unless a seed dies, it bears no fruit, but if it dies it bears much fruit (John 12:24). So he asks to be glorified by his dying and then, of course, in verse 5, by his rising. He wants God to be honoured as he dies and rises. He wants people to get eternal life through his dying and through his rising. The definition of eternal life given in this passage is that you know God and you know Jesus (verse 3). This may be the verse which helped the great John Knox become a Christian. When Knox was dying he asked his wife, 'Read to me where I first cast anchor,' and she read to him from John 17. Eternal life, according to verse 3, does not mean that you know about Jesus – everyone in this building knows about Jesus – it means that you know *him*. It means that you'll one day come face to face and he'll say, 'I know you.' It means that you've welcomed him, you've given him a home in your heart (John 14) and he will give you a home in his glory. Eternal life doesn't mean you get new life beginning after you die, which is the way so many unbelievers think. Eternal life means that you get new life before you die and through your death and on into eternity. So no wonder it is totally proper for Jesus to pray that he'll be glorified, because the Father will be glorified and people will receive eternal life.

Now, friends, when Jesus died, was he glorified? It must have been an excruciating thing to watch. I did a little reading recently on what crucifixion was like. I'd always thought people were crucified high up in the air and you could hardly see it; you could almost walk past without noticing it. But I gather that people were crucified often just a foot above the ground. And there they were with no dignity whatsoever in terrible discomfort. It must have been excruciating, not just to endure, but to watch. Was he glorified as he was crucified? Well, the answer is no doubt, 'Yes.' What bursts out of the cross is: this God *must* be loving and just. There's no sweeping of sin under the carpet here. It is being graphically dealt with. And this God must be wise because he's doing what nobody in the world can do which is to bring a perfect God and sinful people together. This God must be powerful because millions and millions of people are going to live for eternity through this event taking place at Calvary. The prayer that Jesus would be glorified in his death was wonderfully answered. The cross screams the glory of God: his love, wisdom, power, and justice. And when it gets explained, the power of the gospel changes the way people think, understand and, God willing, live (1 Corinthians 1).

I don't know if you've read *Preaching the Whole Bible as Christian Scripture* by Graeme Goldsworthy[1]. There is a diagram in the book which is worth 10,000 words. It's just a little line joining the Old Testament text and the twenty-first-century listener, and on the line between the text and the listener is a cross. Graeme Goldsworthy says if we are going to teach the Old Testament unhelpfully we will just take the text and, like a sky rocket, we'll arch over to the twenty-first-century listener and end up moralizing. For example, 'David killed Goliath; are you brave? Jonah ran away; are you a coward?' Goldsworthy explains that what we must do is follow the time line from the Old Testament across the line and see what Jesus has done to change everything about that message. So we'll find ourselves saying something which is absolutely wonderful, transforming, moving from law to grace, moving from morality, which is so oppressive and wearying for the church, into security and thanksgiving. And so we might find ourselves saying something like this: 'God enabled David to kill Goliath which blessed the whole nation of Israel. Has anything been done since to bless the world with freedom?' The wonderful answer is that what Jesus has done has opened up this tremendous freedom, not just for the nation of Israel, but for the world.

God pursued Jonah and stayed with him even though he was a reluctant messenger. He didn't give up on him and he made sure that Nineveh, a fairly nasty city, heard the message and was given an opportunity to repent. Where's that compassion to be found today? Follow the line: the Son of God loves people like us who are quite nasty, reluctant, unworthy and self-pre-occupied. He demonstrated huge compassion at the cross for people like us. So, in other words, we must keep preaching the cross in all the freshness of the 10,000 texts of the Old Testament so that our people go away saying, 'Thank God for Jesus,' which liberates them to live for him.

So when Jesus prayed for his own glory essentially he was saying, 'Father, make the cross a message which is unstoppably wonderful, as fresh as ten thousand texts, and then glorify me in the resurrection, restore me to the glory that I had with you before the foundation of the world.' This is what governed his mind. And this is what must govern our minds as we pray and as we seek our priorities. There must be a desire for the glory of Jesus which governs what we say, pray and do. All to the glory of Jesus! (John 14)

Jesus' prayer for the apostles

So there is Jesus' prayer for himself. Now his prayer for the apostles is the long bit in verses 6–19. What a mixed bunch they are, and yet he prays that they will be useful, and his prayer was answered. God works through frail instruments. That's one of the wonderful things you must keep reminding yourself. As the Puritans used to say, 'The Lord can draw a straight line with a crooked stick.' So Jesus prays for the apostles. He says that only one has been lost, so we know he's talking about the eleven apostles (verse 12). And just as he had two requests for himself – that he would be glorified *in the hour* and that he would be finally glorified *with the Father* – he now has two requests for the apostles. The first request is that they'd be kept or protected. 'Father, protect them,' in verses 11 and 15. And then he prays that they would be sanctified in verses 17 and 19.

Why is Jesus so narrow in his prayer? Why doesn't he immediately start praying for the world? Why does he specifically say in verse 9, 'I am not praying for the world'? Doesn't God love the world? I want you to notice the sequence. Jesus is praying that the eleven are *kept and sanctified* for their role of preaching and faithfulness, and this is going to impact the world. He wants the world to believe (verse 21); he wants the world to know (verse 23). These eleven, if they are *kept and sanctified*, are going to be the microphone which will start spreading the gospel, reaching hundreds of thousands, and in the next two thousand years going right round the world. What Jesus prayed was the wisest thing in the world to pray for.

Jesus is not praying that the disciples will be kept from trouble; he knows that most of them would be martyred. He wants them to be kept from the world (verse 11) and the devil (verse 15). 'Whatever happens to their bodies,' Jesus might be saying, 'guard their souls.' I think this is a rebuke to our trivial prayers and the way we pray for loved ones. When we live in reasonably good circumstances we can easily absorb all the middle class bourgeois trivia of the world around us. And we find ourselves praying that our children would be happy and successful, although we don't put it quite as boldly as that. We are praying for something that is just a little different from what a pagan might be praying. You see the sting of this? Do you want your children to be just successful and happy? What about wanting your child to be *kept and sanctified* so that even if he or she gets martyred before they reach thirty-five years old, God is glorified? That's a brave prayer; that's a Bible prayer.

And in verse 11 Jesus prays specifically that the Father will keep them 'by the power of your name' which, of course, you know means his character. Jesus is praying that the Father would keep the apostles by his faithful character, and God answered this prayer. All the evidence we have is that the eleven apostles were kept right to the end, and they were sanctified for the task. I want to suggest to you that the twosome that he is praying for the apostles, *kept and sanctified*, has not properly entered our bloodstream. One of the things I would really hope from this particular talk is that there will be some of you, maybe many of you, who will take these two words, 'kept' and 'sanctified', and make them part of your prayer life. So that when you're thinking of friends and you're not quite sure what to say, pray, 'Keep them, sanctify them.' And when you're thinking of your pastor and you don't know what to say, pray, 'Father, keep him, sanctify him.' When you're thinking of missionaries in a very difficult context pray, 'Keep them, sanctify them.' And as this prayer goes up to the Father, who is so gracious to hear our prayers, what do you think might happen? The Father hears the prayer, a thousand darts that are being aimed at that guy, that lady, are diverted as we've prayed. The temptation that is going to face them down the street finds no great interest in them. God is at work; the sinful impulse we've all got which is looking for an outlet and sometimes prowls around looking for a way to indulge, gets no opportunity. The things of Jesus suddenly appear to be very great and very wonderful, and the things of the world suddenly look very little and very temporary because the Father has heard somebody pray, 'Keep them, sanctify them.' It's a wonderful prayer, such a powerful appeal. I hope you'll put it into your head and heart as you pray and take a leaf out of Jesus' prayer life. He modelled this prayer and it tells us what's important to him.

Now what does it mean to be sanctified? There are two ways God sanctifies. One way is to get into position, to be set apart. It's like picking a special team: 'We're going to sanctify a group for a particular task. So let's set so-and-so apart for this particular job, let's commit them, let's devote them, let's sanctify them for this task.' As 1 Corinthians 6:11 says, 'You were sanctified,' set apart for Jesus. The other way that God sanctifies is to make people holy in a process. It's the process of being transformed into the likeness of Christ; it's the steady change that God works in us so people become more and more like the character of the Lord Jesus. 'May they grow in Christlikeness,' that's what we are praying. 'Sanctify their nature.'

In 1 Thessalonians 5:23 Paul writes, 'May God . . . sanctify you,' but he writes to the Corinthians, 'You are sanctified.' He could have written to the Corinthians, 'May God sanctify you.' He could have written to the Thessalonians, 'You are sanctified.' Position or process – now which is it here? Does Jesus want them to be in position, or does he want them to make progress? I think it's most likely the first, and I say that on the basis of verse 19 where Jesus says, 'I sanctify myself.' We know straight away that he is not improving himself, he's not wanting progress in his character, he's not wanting the process of sanctification, the likeness of God to improve, he's positioning himself. Where's his position going to be? Well, first of all it's going to be at the cross. 'I put myself in position so that they may be sanctified. I am going to go to where I *should be*, the cross, so that they will be where they *can be* which is in your family.'

So put the two requests together. They are the two sides of the same coin: 'Father, keep the apostles from a thousand dangers. Father, sanctify them for one great purpose.' Isn't that a wonderful prayer? And again just think how God might answer this. We're no good at getting people to change: we can't get our family to change, we can't get some relatives to change, we can't get neighbours to change, we can't get parishioners to change, we can't get pastors to change, we can't get bishops to change. We're hugely limited, aren't we? Here is a brilliant prayer and it's not too big a burden. I'm not trying to burden you. I'm not saying, 'Please go and be a praying hero.' I want this to free you; I want you to rejoice about this. I want you to see what Jesus prayed, how brilliant it is, and use it as a great key.

Now what's going to keep the apostles in position is the truth. They need to be clear in their minds what they are doing, who they are, why they are there, what their job is. They need the truth. Verse 17: 'Sanctify them by the truth.' Friends, this is not the truth that you and I want to believe, this is not the truth that the confused world tells us to believe, this is the truth which Jesus has been talking about in John 14:15–16, where the Spirit will enable the apostles to record the truth, the words of Jesus, the life of Jesus, and they will find themselves with an Old and New Testament. That truth is going to keep them for the task, so they know who they are, why they are there, what they are doing, why they're doing it and where it's all going to finish. That's what we need: we need to learn the truth if we are to do our task in the world.

Jesus' prayer for all believers

Well, in our last few minutes, let's look at the prayer for all believers in verses 17–26. Jesus is interceding for all the believers down through the history of the world, including us, and again he has two requests. He had two requests for himself, 'Father, glorify me in the hour, glorify me with you back home' (author's translation). He had two requests for the apostles, 'Keep them,' 'Sanctify them.' And now he has two requests for believers like us, 'that all of them would be one' (verse 21) and that they would one day be in glory (verse 24). Isn't it wonderful that Jesus prayed that we would be in glory? Don't you wonder sometimes whether you will ever be in glory? Do you wonder sometimes whether there is a glory? Jesus prays for them to be taken to glory. Every single prayer he has prayed has been answered. He prayed for himself to be glorified on the cross: he was; he prayed to be glorified back with the Father: he was; he prayed for the apostles to be kept: they were; he prayed for the apostles to be sanctified: they were. He now prays that we'll be one and we'll get home to glory.

However, very importantly, our unity is in the truth (verse 20). We need to belong to the same apostolic message, that's why we need to keep humbly reading our Bible. Let's sit under our Bibles, let's be open to the correction of the Bible. God has made us one family by his Spirit. We may disagree on lots of things, but we are one family. How are we going to be united in mind and heart? By sitting under the Bible and by reading it humbly together. The Word of God is going to make us a mature family, not just a united family. We're not just going to be united in the Spirit, we're going to be united in the truth.

I suspect that's what verse 22 is about: 'I have given them the glory that you gave me, that they may be one as we are one.' Jesus is saying here, 'I've given them the revelation of myself, I've shown them what I think, I've shown them what I say, and I've shown them what I do. I've given them the glory, the revelation.'

But this unity is not just going to be in truth, it's going to be relational, as Jesus explains in verse 21, 'Father, just as you are in me and I am in you. May they also be in us.' Friends, the bonds that we have here may be very superficial. You and I may have a quick conversation; you think to yourself, 'How fast can I get away from this guy?' But in a thousand years we'll have a fellowship which will be so close, so special, so rich, so perfect, we won't believe it. That's what God's begun: relational unity. And the unity also is going to be progressive. In verse 23 Jesus prays, 'May they be brought to complete unity.' This is not just spiritual unity but being one in mind and heart as the Scriptures are heeded.

Kathy and I are about to head home in a few days. We are going to go via Vancouver. We're going to visit her brother who is a pastor there. He's had to fight a very, very difficult battle for the last couple of years. The leadership of the Anglican Church there has basically said, 'We are not going to listen to the Bible on controversial issues. We're going to listen to the street, what the world tells us, that's what we'll listen to.' So my brother-in-law stood to protest with a number of others and they have had their licences taken away. Jim Packer was on staff and he's had his licence taken away; buildings have been locked; whole congregations have been made homeless and have to find a building to meet in. But the believers, under the sovereign hand of God, are rejoicing, absolutely rejoicing. They see the issues, they love the Lord, they are united in the truth, they are united in the Spirit, they are indwelt by the Spirit, they're surrendered to the Scriptures, and they're thriving. They've had more young people applying for the ministry in the last few years than they've had in the last twenty years.

Well, finally, Jesus says he's praying that they might all arrive with him (verse 24). Why are we going to arrive? Because Jesus went through with the crucifixion (chapter 14). 'I go to prepare a place.' He did it, he prepared a place. He didn't prepare a place for good people, he didn't prepare a place for successful people, he prepared a place for believers. And I want to show you something very interesting as we finish in verse 24. He doesn't say, 'Father, I'm asking.' Do you notice the word? It's, 'Father, I want,' and the phrase in the original is, *I will it*. 'Father, I will it. I'm telling you what my will is.' Isn't that an incredible thing? Jesus says, 'I'm telling you what the will is. I will that they be with me.'

So, brothers and sisters, keep carrying the torch. There's a little Olympic torch travelling around this country, but there's a mighty torch you're carrying round the country. You may only be going a few hundred metres, but your few hundred metres is very wonderful. Keep carrying the torch. When Lloyd-Jones was at the very end of his life, he'd got to the age of eighty one and he was obviously dying. His family and friends gathered round. Many people thought they should be praying urgently for a miracle, because if Lloyd-Jones died how could they possibly survive? And Lloyd-Jones apparently wrote a shaky little note to his wife telling them not to pray for a miracle because he didn't want to be kept from glory.

Notes

1. Graeme Goldsworthy, *Preaching the Whole Bible as Christian Scripture* (Inter-Varsity Press / Eerdmans, 2000).

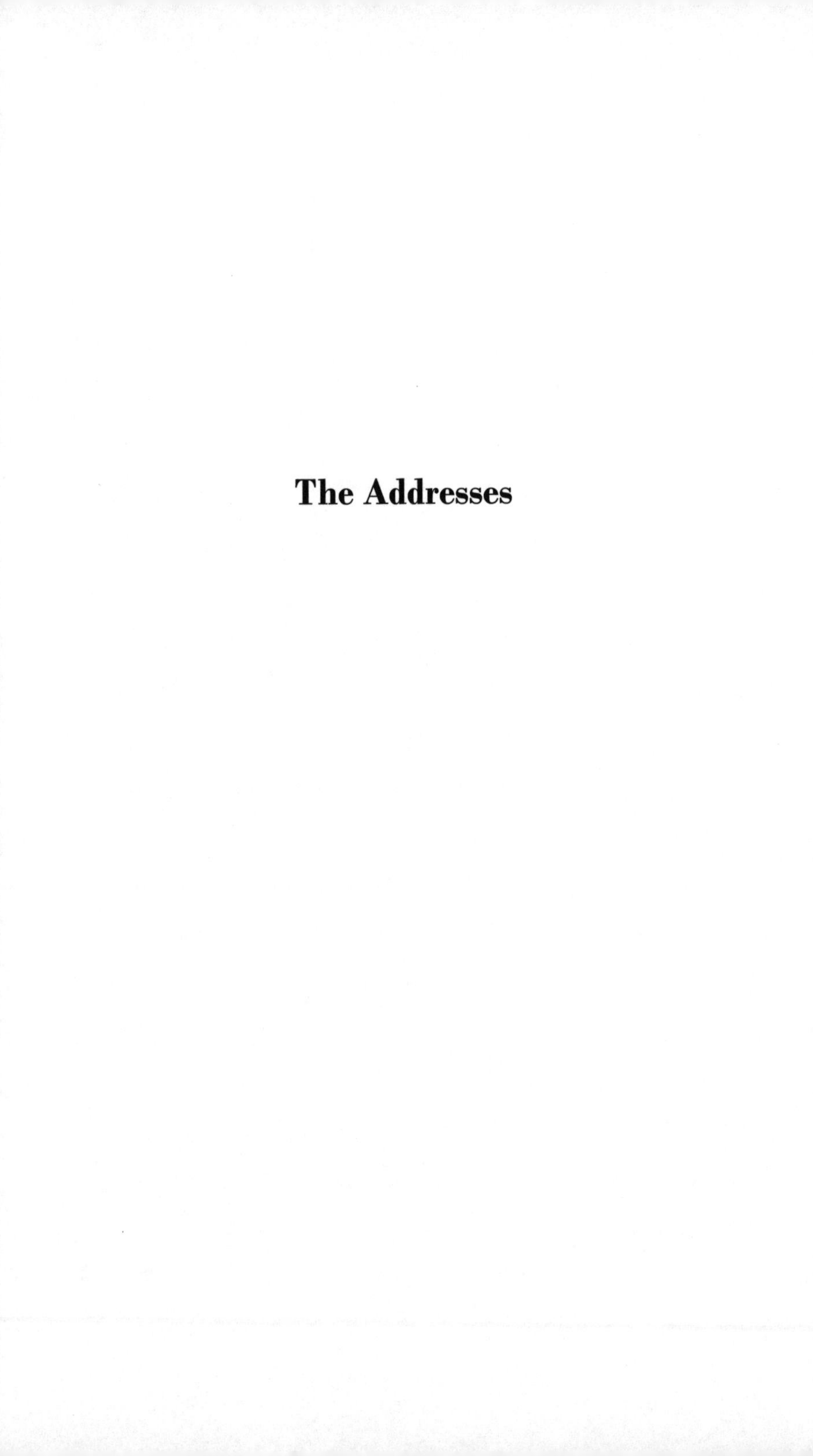

The Addresses

Creation Struck Down

by Christopher Ash

Christopher serves as Director of the Proclamation Trust's Cornhill Training Course in London. He is married to Carolyn and they have three sons, a daughter, and two grandsons. Christopher is an author and, before coming to London, was a church pastor in East Anglia.

Creation Struck Down: Genesis 3

Friends, I would love you to tell me about your family. In a gathering this size there would be many stories to tell. Some would be wonderful stories. I would love to tell you of my dad, who landed with the first wave of Allied troops on D-Day and won a Military Cross. He's still alive. I would be proud to tell you that story.

But there would be other stories of which we are ashamed, of parents, grandparents, more distant ancestors, who had done cowardly things, ugly things, evil things. Those stories affect us too.

This evening I need to tell you an older story about my family. It is a story of which I am deeply ashamed. And it is your story too. It is the story of our first ancestors. It is a true story. Part of me wishes it had not been told. But it must be told. For only when it is heard can it be healed. If we want to live in the light of the future, we must first face up to where we are in the light of the past. We must tell the story of Genesis 3.

It's a very well-known story, almost too well-known. It's going to answer for us three questions. Firstly, why am I mortal – why do I get sick, why does my hair go grey, why do I grow old and die? Secondly, why am I sinful – why are there ugly desires and thoughts in my mind and on my heart? Thirdly, what will it take for me to be rescued, changed and given hope?

I'm going to retell the story in four scenes and then come back to those questions. But before I do that, I want us to look at Romans 5:12, the most important New Testament commentary on Genesis 3: 'Sin entered the world through one man, and death through sin, and in this way death came to all people, because all sinned.' Paul tells us three important things here. First, that sin entered the world through one man. That historical event, when the first man in human history sinned, opened the gate for sin to enter the world. Second, death entered the world through, and because of, sin. Third that, 'in this way death came to all people, because all sinned'. Paul is saying something very precise here. He is not saying that we die because Adam sinned, in some way disconnected from us, as if Adam sinned and we are quite arbitrarily sentenced to death because of his sin. Nor is he saying that we die because we happened to sin, but if we managed not to, we would not die. As if Adam just set us a bad example and it's a shame that we follow it; but, of course, if anybody managed not to follow it they'd be fine. No, he says, 'in this way' death came to all people, so there is a connection between Adam's sin and our sin.

He is saying that we sin because Adam sinned, and that's why we die. We die because we are sinners. But we are sinners, not just because we happen to follow Adam's example. No, we are sinners because sin entered the world through Adam. Human nature was poisoned at its source. This is what theologians call original sin, that is, sin that goes right back to our origins. From that terrible day onwards, the only kind of child that Adam and Eve could procreate would be a sinner like them.

In the 1950s there was an eccentric estate agent in London called Roy Brooks who decided to sell properties by telling the unvarnished truth about them in small ads in *The Sunday Times*. My favourite is, 'Don't be misled by the exterior – it's worse inside.' That's what it is to be a human being. Our exteriors vary, in many ways, but it is worse inside. The human heart is poisoned with a poison that entered the human race at its source.

What is more, every part of my humanness is touched and spoiled by sin. This is the doctrine of total depravity. This doctrine doesn't say that human beings are as evil as we could possibly be; that would make us demons and is patently not true. It means that every part of us is spoiled by sin. Some years ago, my wife set about brightening up the house front by buying a wooden flower tub. It had been made by sawing an old whisky barrel in two. I was tasked with drilling drainage holes in the base. As I did so, there was an unmistakeable smell of whisky! Every part of the wood was soaked in whisky. In the same way, every part of our humanity is soaked in sin.

My mind cannot think right because I am sinful. My feelings and emotions are not right because I am sinful. My affections, what I desire, what I hate, are disordered because I am sinful. So with that introduction, let us hear again the true story of our first ancestors.

Scene 1: The Great Deception (verses 1–5)

'Now the snake was more crafty than any of the wild animals the LORD God had made.' The snake is a creature, not a rival god. God made the snake crafty. In some deep way it was necessary that there be this crafty creature. He is called in Scripture a snake, a dragon, the sea-monster Leviathan, Satan, the devil, a murderer and the father of lies. We're not told why he came to be there. We are told his character: 'crafty', deceitful.

You will notice that he doesn't come up to the woman hissing and spitting, like a cobra about to strike: 'I am a monster and I am going to steal your paradise, your innocence, your happiness and ruin them all.' Eve would have run a mile. Instead, he's like one of those cuddly, soft toy snakes. He sits on the bench near her and engages her in conversation. Notice the three strands to his great deception: the first strand to his deception is *God is not good* – he can't be trusted; he wants to deprive you of something good; he is deliberately holding back the best. The second strand is *God is not dangerous* – you will not certainly die. Disobedience is not as serious as that. God is not the sort of God who kills people. I know he said it but he doesn't actually mean it. He's just a great big teddy bear in the sky, he won't mind. He loves everybody, doesn't he? The third strand to the lie is *You will be like God*. The snake promises Eve the knowledge of good and evil or 'wisdom' (verse 6). You will know things that are meant to be hidden from human beings, things that only God should know.

That is the great deception, the most successful trio of lies in human history, and it's going strong today. God is not good; God is not dangerous; and we can be like God. The snake is wrong about God; he is wrong about judgment; he is wrong about human beings. But we so want to believe him and so did Eve.

This deception leads straight into:

Scene 2: The Great Disobedience (verse 6)

In quick succession five things happen: four by Eve, one by Adam.

1. Eve saw 'that the fruit of the tree was good for food' – it pleases the appetite; 'and pleasing to the eye' – it appeals to the desire of the heart; and 'desirable for gaining wisdom' – that's the big one, becoming like God.
2. 'She took some' – she acted on the desire of her eyes.
3. 'She ate it.'

4. Because it is in the nature of sin to draw in others (sin is infectious) Eve also 'gave some to her husband'. Adam was evidently present but passive, abdicating his responsibility to care and lead.
5. 'He ate it.' The Bible says that is the defining moment in human history, when Adam sinned. The good order of creation is turned upside down. The woman listens to the snake; the man submits to the woman. And sin entered the world through one man.

The great disobedience is immediately followed by:

Scene 3: The Great Disappointment (verses 7–8)

In quick succession five more things happen.

1. 'The eyes of both of them were opened.' But what do they see?
2. 'They realized they were naked.' At the end of chapter 2 they were naked but felt no shame. Now they feel shame. For the first time in human history a man and a woman feel the shame of a guilty conscience.
3. 'So they sewed fig leaves together and made coverings for themselves.' The word means an inadequate loincloth, not much more than a belt. Not, I think, to hide from one another, but to hide from God. Up till now, God has provided all their needs. But to hide from God they have to use their own resources.

4. They heard 'the LORD God as he was walking in the garden'. The sound which previously would have filled them with delight now fills them with fear.
5. 'They hid from the LORD God among the trees.' All is now masks, hypocrisy, pretending, covering up. They believed the deception; they become deceivers.

Their eyes were opened; they realized they were naked; they sewed; they made coverings; they heard; and they hid.

The father of lies makes the great deception. The father of sinners commits the great disobedience. The human race is consigned to the great disappointment.

And then:

Scene 4: The Dawn of Hope (verses 9–24)

What happens is a question, a blaming, three curses, a provision and an expulsion.

A question (verses 9–11)

'The LORD God called to the man, "Where are you?"' God takes the initiative to seek the lost. He asks the question, not because he doesn't know. This is like a mum or dad playing hide-and-seek with their child calling out, 'Where are you?' when, of course, they know perfectly well where the child is. God calls because it's not the end of the story.

Blaming (verses 12–13)

God said (verse 11), 'Who told you that you were naked?

Have you eaten from the tree that I commanded you not to eat from?' Again, it's not that God doesn't know. He knows, but it needs to be brought into the open if salvation is to begin. And then the blaming begins. The man blames the woman and the woman blames the snake. Why is our instinct to blame others? We do it because Adam and Eve did it and bequeathed to us that sinful nature.

Curses (verses 14–19)

Then there were three curses, three necessary entailments of human disobedience. First, the curse on the snake in verses 14–15. The snake is cursed, figuratively, to be a dust-eating, earth-bound creature and cursed to hostility with the offspring of the woman. In the end, her offspring will 'crush your head and you will strike his heel'. The two words are the same, but their effect is quite different. One is directed to the heel: it will hurt, it will cause harm, but it will not give victory. The other is directed to the snake's head. The day will come when the Serpent-crusher will destroy death and him who has the power of death, that is, the devil. And in that curse there is gospel.

The disaster that began with the snake will end with the crushing of the snake. And so the story that began with the father of lies and continued with the father of sinners will end with the God and Father of the Lord Jesus Christ, the Father who planned salvation long before he even created the world. The Father is not reacting to unexpected events; he is working out his eternal purpose.

Then comes the curse on the woman in verse 16. This is a curse that hurts her in her most wonderful role, the procreator of new life on earth. There will be new life but it will come through pain at the start as a sign that it will come through pain at every stage. And 'your desire will be for your husband': the same phrase, word for word, is used in chapter 4:7, where it means, 'desire to master, desire to dominate, desire to take charge'. That is probably the meaning here. The godly, ordered, harmonious relations of men and women are to be disordered and part of that disorder is the woman wanting to dominate. And the flip-side is 'he will rule over you', his godly servant leadership replaced by a selfish male chauvinism. From that day relations between men and women become distorted into arrogant, pushy feminism on the one hand and arrogant, abusive male chauvinism on the other.

In verses 17–19 the man is cursed. This curse focuses on Adam's role as farmer and gardener. Because you listened to your wife rather than obeying God, 'cursed is the ground because of you'. Work becomes toil; achievement is mocked by frustration; life is dogged by pointlessness and emptiness. And, finally, there is disintegration: 'dust you are and to dust you will return' (verse 19). You will die. The snake says you won't, but you will. In the day you eat the fruit you die, you become mortal, you come under sentence of death, you begin to age, and you will die.

Why is Adam mortal? Because Adam is sinful.

Questions, blaming, curses, and then . . .

Provision (verses 20–21)

Adam calls his wife 'Eve', probably a wordplay or pun on the Hebrew word for 'life'. She will become the mother of all the living. Although under sentence of death, there will still be a human race. The story is not over. And 'The LORD God made garments . . . for Adam and his wife and clothed them.' The word means long tunics down to the knees or ankles. What a contrast to the inadequate man-made loin-cloths of verse 7! Even before the expulsion from the garden, God provides for their protection.

Questions, blaming, curses, provision, but finally expulsion:

Expulsion (verses 22–24)

In verse 22, God says that Adam 'has now become like one of us, knowing good and evil'. In some way, he has grasped for knowledge and got knowledge he ought not to have. 'He must not be allowed to reach out his hand and take also from the tree of life and live forever.' God is not being insecure here, defensively protecting his privileges. No, God knows that the universe will disintegrate if he allows a rival power to live forever. The integrity of the universe depends on the uniqueness of the one true God. There must be one supreme power and one alone.

And so, as a mark of his grace (verse 23), 'He banished him from the Garden of Eden . . . After he drove the man out, he placed on the east side of the Garden of Eden cherubim and a flaming sword flashing back and forth to guard the way to the tree of life.' There will be no return until God opens the way. All down the history of the Old Testament they put pictures of cherubim and trees on the tabernacle in the wilderness and on the temple in Jerusalem. As if to say, 'You cannot go in, the garden is closed; and yet one day the curtain will be torn in two and Paradise will be yours again.'

And becoming aware of this barrier is the first step to becoming a Christian. The human condition is desperately serious. I am mortal – I get sick, I grow old, I die – because I am sinful. I am sinful because Adam sinned and I have Adam's nature. So I sin; my sin is my fault and my responsibility. I cannot escape my sinful nature. It is not in my power. And while I have this sinful nature, I must be excluded from Paradise.

So let's ask our three questions. Why am I mortal? Because I am sinful. Why am I sinful? I have a sinful nature inherited from Adam. What will it take for me to have hope? Now we can answer this.

So what is needed?

What is needed for you and for me to have life? For our mortality to be healed, our sin forgiven and our hearts changed? What is needed is a new Adam and a new humanity. Because the human race is poisoned at source, we need a new source. We need a man who is fully human, who feels the full deceitfulness of the father of lies, and yet who is fully obedient in life and in death. We need a man who does not consider equality with God a thing to be grasped; a man who by his death for sinners bears our curse; a man who by his death destroys him who has the power of death, that is, the devil. And what is needed is for you and for me to have a new birth into that new humanity.

Implications

If you and I are to go the distance with Jesus Christ, we need to hear the story of our ancestors. We need to resist any pseudo-Christianity that takes a short-cut around Genesis 3 and becomes unrealistic and shallow about our sinful natures.

When we hear Genesis 3, it will help us in at least three ways.

It will make us realistic about our old nature

We will remember that, even though by grace we are forgiven and justified by the blood of Jesus, and by grace the Holy Spirit dwells in our hearts, nevertheless the old nature remains and will do till we die or the Lord returns. My instinct is still to put myself at the centre. My first reaction is still to blame someone else. My conscience naturally accuses me. Every morning I need fresh grace to keep me. In the words of the old eighteenth-century hymn by Robert Robinson, 'Prone to wander, Lord, I feel it, prone to leave the God I love; Here's my heart, O take and seal it, seal it for Thy courts above.'

It will save me from shallow perversions of Christianity

I was talking to someone a couple of weeks ago and asking him what he thinks Christianity is. 'It makes me feel better about myself,' was the substance of his answer. Jesus as the self-help guru, the lifestyle coach, the consultant who puts me on the couch for a while and then I go out with my head held high. But Christianity is not a programme to make me feel better about myself.

Genesis 3 tells me that sin came into the world through one man, and death through sin and so death came to all people, because all people sinned. And until there is a Second Adam, and until he dies for sinners, and until I am born again into his humanity, there is no hope for me. Genesis 3 tells me I need the message of God's unmerited grace, that is made possible by Christ's atoning death, and that gives me new birth and a changed heart. Don't settle for anything less.

And never mistake Christianity for a programme of social improvement for the world. Yes, Christianity does make the world a better place, a much better place, thank God. But that is not what Christianity is. Christianity is about the cross of Christ, about a radical new birth by the Spirit, about being transferred by God from the old human race in Adam to the redeemed human race in Christ. Genesis 3 shows me that nothing less than this can offer hope.

It will fill my heart with wonder, love and praise for Jesus

How wonderful that God sent a second Adam. A man just like you and me, fully human, tempted as we are. Equality with God was dangled before him by the snake as something to be grasped and yet he did not grasp it but humbled himself. A man who, by his death for sinners, became our curse for us and by that death destroyed him who has the power of death, that is, the devil. Praise God for the Serpent-crusher.

Praise God that because of him, 'The God of peace will soon crush Satan under [our] feet' (Romans 16:20). We cannot crush him. We cannot resist him. By nature we fall for his deception, we repeat the disobedience, we experience the disappointment. And yet in Christ we are not trapped to live in the light of the past. This story which is your story and my story must be told but in Christ it is being healed.

Time and Eternity

by Mike Raiter

Mike is the Director of the Centre for Biblical Preaching, a partnership of the Church Missionary Society and St James' Old Cathedral in Melbourne, Australia. He is married to Sarah and they have four children. After beginning his working life as a high school teacher, and completing his theological education, he taught at the Zarephath Bible Institute in Pakistan. Following his return to Australia he established the Department of Mission at Moore College in Sydney.

Time and Eternity: Ecclesiastes 3:1–22

Unmasking the clichés

I left South East Asia to return to Australia in 1997. I'd been involved in theological education for a few years and for the last year served as the interim principal of a small but important Bible college. The college had been training men and women for Christian ministry for about fifteen years. We came home and my colleague returned from his twelve-month furlough and resumed the reins of principal.

The new academic year began in August. But it was only a week or two before problems emerged. One of the new students had had some involvement in national politics and decided to use his political skills in the college. He formed a little party amongst the students and began to agitate for change. Then one day in class one of the students, a

Muslim convert, made some indiscrete comments about the Christian community. These comments so enraged this other student, the politician, that he threatened to kill the convert and actually had to be physically restrained from doing so.

This attempted murder, plus his politicking, convinced the faculty that this man wouldn't make an ideal pastor and he was expelled. He refused to leave, so his family and pastor were summoned from 150 miles away to come and take him home. They came but he still refused to leave. By this time his party of mainly first-year students had been persuaded to support him. The situation was a standoff, and so the principal closed the college.

The police were called in to escort the students off the campus. Within three weeks of the new academic year an effective training institution was closed. I wish I could say that this was an unusual blight on an otherwise impeccable history. I wish I could say that most of our students were nothing like this. But the fact is that despite years of Bible teaching and modelling godly living, we saw very little change in behaviour in many of our students.

I remember my colleague said to me on one occasion, after a particularly nasty outbreak of fighting, 'I really wonder if we achieve anything here or are we just wasting our time?' I'd always been taught that if you faithfully preach the gospel then you'll see fruit. Well, I wish it were that simple. We didn't see a lot of fruit. In fact, we saw a lot of frustration, discouragement and failure but not too much success.

Elisabeth Elliot tells the story of her early years working in Ecuador amongst the Colorado Indians. For nine months she studied the language, providing the tools that would one day make possible the translation of the Bible into this language. She put all her handwritten notes and files on the top of a bus to be typed up in the city. The bus arrived but no notes. The whole lot had disappeared from the top of the bus. Nine months of work irretrievably lost. What a waste!

A little later she heard from her fiancé, Jim Elliot. He'd spent two years rebuilding a small mission station: repairing three buildings and constructing two new ones. A flood came and in an instant two years' work was washed away. What a waste! As Elisabeth thought about why the sovereign God would allow this, she said there was no light, no echo, no possible explanation. The reality is, if we're honest about life, there's a great deal we do which seems to be a waste of time. Life is full of perplexities and conundrums and, no matter how faithful and prayerful and godly you might be, you'll face failure and frustration.

I remember talking to a friend some years ago about quiet times. She made the point that she always has to have her quiet time because the day never seems to go right unless she's had it. I've heard that many times: 'When I have my quiet time it just makes a difference to the day.'

I wonder if Elisabeth Elliot had her quiet time the morning nine months' worth of work disappeared from the top of a bus? I wonder what kind of quiet time my colleague had the day he closed the Bible college and saw his ministry come to a standstill? It would be nice if we lived in a world where, when you have your quiet time, everything's rosy and when you don't, things go wrong. But we don't live in a world like that. I, like you, have had days when I didn't have a quiet time, or had a perfunctory one, and the day's been perfectly fine. And I've had days when my time with the Lord was rich and precious and the day's been a shocker. And it makes you wonder, what's the point? Perhaps it's true after all: meaningless, meaningless, all is meaningless.

Times and seasons

We're looking in these evenings at a book which deals with the confusion, futility, absurdity and the meaninglessness of life. It's about how one responds when nothing in your life makes sense and you're perplexed and bewildered. That's the book and the world of Ecclesiastes.

Let's briefly dip back into the book. In chapter 1:14 the Teacher draws this depressing conclusion from his observation of everything: I have seen all the things that are done under the sun and have found everything to be futile. More knowledge just brings more grief. Pleasure is futile. Laughter is madness. All one's achievements amount to nothing. And the end of all your labour – whether starting a business, planting a church, coaching a football team – you finish and pass on your life's work to someone else who turns out to be an incompetent nincompoop. And your business goes bust, your church is empty, and your football team are relegated. What's the point? And so chapter 2 ends on the cheery note: this too is futile and a pursuit of the wind.

And our Teacher's despair increases as we move into chapter 3 and look at God's ordering of the world. In probably the most famous section of the book, the Teacher reminds us that there's a time for everything under heaven, that is, across the whole expanse of life in this world. You see, the Teacher doesn't draw some neat distinction between life in the church and life in the world, or life in relationship with the Lord or life apart from the Lord, or the life of the righteous as opposed to the life of the wicked. You miss the whole point of Ecclesiastes if you draw such neat and tidy distinctions; he's describing life *wherever* you look. And in these verses he's really repeating what he said in chapter 1: a generation comes and a generation goes, the sun rises and the sun sets, Keswicks come and Keswicks go. There's birth and death, planting and uprooting, killing and healing, tearing down and building up. He covers the whole gamut of human activities – all ordained by God.

But what's the point he's making? Is he pointing to the wonderful, beautiful diversity of life? Is he reminding us of the sovereignty of God who watches over all the events of our life? No, he tells us in verse 9. What does all this working, weeping, laughing, embracing, searching, sowing, speaking, loving, hating, warring, peacemaking produce? What's the cash value? What do we gain from it all? Well, he's already told us again and again – absolutely nothing.

And he explains this in verses 10–11, two of the most misunderstood verses of the book. The Teacher acknowledges that God has made everything 'beautiful', or better 'appropriate' for its time. The world is the way it is because God has ordered it this way. This endless cycle of life is God's doing. And to rub salt into the wound, God has put an awareness of this into people's hearts. The word which is translated 'eternity' really means an awareness of the past and the future, the very thing he's been describing for the past two and a half chapters. He's saying that God has consigned this world to futility, frustration and endless monotony. And our pain and despair is heightened by the fact that we can see that. Small children love merry-go-rounds and in their innocence they can go around and around and never grow tired of seeing the same thing. But an adult soon realizes that the merry-go-round is endlessly going nowhere and sees the futility of the whole exercise. All we see as we sit on the merry-go-round of life is the same: the same scenes, the same activities, the same sameness. A few years ago, the then Premier of New South Wales in Australia, Bob Carr, made a comment that formed the next day's headline. There'd been a terrible murder/suicide in Sydney and he said, 'Life is an inherently disappointing experience for most human beings. Some people can't cope with that.'

In the face of this almost overpowering despair, what do we do? Just end it all? Just curl up and die in frustration? The Teacher's solution is to take what enjoyment you can out of this rather sad, pathetic life. Eat, drink, and enjoy yourself because things aren't going to change. He says: I know that all God does will last forever. Nothing we can do is going to make a scrap of difference to that. There's no adding to it or taking away; whatever has already been, and whatever will be, already is (verse 14). And on that note this very unusual book continues for another nine depressing chapters.

Making sense out of the senseless

What are we to make of Ecclesiastes? What are we to do with the Teacher's puzzling, disturbing observations about life? Well, there are a couple of things we can do. One alternative is to explain away his hard statements. We can tie up all the loose ends for him. We can say, 'Yes, life's like that when you don't know Jesus. There is a monotony, dreariness, frustration and confusion but that all changes when you give your life to Jesus; the clouds all disappear, the grey skies turn to blue. When you come to Jesus everything makes sense; you have an answer to every question and a verse for every occasion.' That's one approach to Ecclesiastes. That's what I call the 'God always blesses the quiet time' approach.

Or, we can honestly confront the truth the Teacher throws into our faces again and again. And that is, whether you live a life of belief or unbelief, whether you're in the world or the church, life is still full of uncertainties, perplexities, seeming absurdities and unanswered questions. In the end we must allow the gospel of our risen Saviour to qualify the despairing observations of Ecclesiastes. Indeed, I want to say that there's no book in the Old Testament which more cries out for the gospel than Ecclesiastes. There is no book which more demands another chapter to be written, a gospel chapter, than Ecclesiastes. The Teacher desperately needs to hear the voice of Jesus.

But at the same time we must heed the warning the Teacher is giving us. And his warning is that one of the great threats to mature faith, a threat more subtle than secular atheism, is trite religiosity, bumper-sticker Christianity, the 'God always blesses the quiet time piety'. You hear it all the time: 'We've prayed for Marjory and she's not healed. You can see why. She lacks faith. It's black and white.' Or, 'Scripture says, "Train up a child in the way he should go and he will not depart from it." Look at the Smiths, four children and all off the rails. It's not hard to know why.' That's trite religiosity, black and white Christianity. It'd be nice if life were like that.

But the Teacher tells us that in reality much of life is grey, murky and confusing. Like the writer of Ecclesiastes I have seen worldly Christians who rarely, if ever, read the Bible with their kids or prayed for them, who taught them secular values of success and ambition and each of their three kids have grown up to be godly believers. And I've seen mighty saints of God – prayerful, humble, diligent, faithful – and not one child walking with the Lord. The Teacher will conclude: it's all vanity, a chasing after the wind.

And one must not run away from the fact that life in a fallen world is like that. I remember years ago, after I was ordained, we were required to complete two years of post-ordination training. We called it 'potty training'. A clergyman spoke to us who'd been the pastor of a large, growing church. His ministry was fulfilling and rewarding. He loved life and loved serving God. But he'd had a massive heart attack and was fighting for his life. If he pulled through he'd never run a church again; his heart wouldn't have the strength. A fellow pastor came to visit him in hospital. He was lying there tubes out of everywhere, depressed and angry at God. But the visitor had a word of Scripture for him, 'All things work together for good . . . ' My friend said, 'If I'd had the energy I would have punched him. His ministry wasn't in tatters. He wasn't facing life with a weak heart. The bottom hadn't fallen out of his world. But he had a word of Scripture for me.'

Now of course, it was a true word – and it was a word my friend knew well – but the comment lacked wisdom. There's a time to speak and a time to be quiet and that pastor couldn't tell the time.

It was trite, it was simplistic, it was an inability or refusal to face the fact that a major tragedy had struck a God-fearing man and in the end only God knows why, and he had not revealed it.

You see, Ecclesiastes is one of those important but uncomfortable *Yes but* parts of the Bible.

Proverbs says, if you trust in the Lord your plans will succeed. And then Job says, *Yes, but* there was a man on earth more trusting and obedient than any other, Job, and he suffered indescribably. Proverbs will say, 'The fear of the

Lord prolongs life, but the years of the wicked will be short' (ESV). *Yes but* says Psalm 73, I saw the prosperity of the wicked. They have an easy time until they die, and their bodies are well fed. *Yes but* says Ecclesiastes, I've seen the godly cut down in their prime and the wicked live to a ripe old age and die peacefully in their sleep. The Teacher is saying, don't take what are meant to be general observations of life and turn them into cheap bumper stickers which reduce life in a fallen world to trite simplicity. And that's why we must read the books of wisdom together. Job isn't the whole story, or Ecclesiastes, or Proverbs, but read together they are the pathway to wisdom.

Ecclesiastes and the gospel

The Teacher's observations on life reflect the frustration and absurdity of life in a fallen world. But, of course, much more has been revealed to us. The Teacher asks: who knows if the spirit of people rises upward and the body goes to the earth? And we cry out, 'We know because the Lord Jesus rose from the dead.' The Teacher will ask: what does a man get for all his work and all his efforts that he labours at under the sun? And we reply with the apostle Paul, in the light of the gospel, 'Therefore, my dear brothers and sisters, stand firm. Let nothing move you. Always give yourselves fully to the work of the Lord, because you know that your labour in the Lord is not in vain' (1 Corinthians 15:58). In frustration the Teacher will say: man cannot discover the work God has done from beginning to end. But Paul says: 'For now we see only a reflection as in a mirror; but then face to face. Now I know in part; but then I will know fully, even as I am fully known' (1 Corinthians 13:12).

The world view of Ecclesiastes lies behind Paul's words in Romans 8:20: for the creation was subjected to futility – to meaninglessness, absurdity – not of its own will but by the will of the one who subjected it in hope. Paul agrees with the Teacher: yes, there is a sense in which the great defining mark of this world, this life, is futility and frustration. But God has subjected this world in the certain hope of the glorious liberation of the sons of God. It's as if the trees, the clouds, the mountains and the seas that are locked into this endless, monotonous cycle of life know that in a little while they'll throw the shackles of their futile ways and be set free to become a new liberated creation. And we, too, look forward to that day. In the meantime computers will crash and three years' work on a PhD will be lost. The wiring in the newly completed church building will catch fire and it'll burn to the ground. Or the young man in whose life and spiritual growth you've invested months and months will just get up and walk away. And you'll think of the days you sacrificed time with your own kids to be with him – and all for nothing.

But we know a day is coming, a day of justice, a day when the greys will become white, when the mist is blown away and we understand. But until then we live with frustration and with perplexity.

Fear God

As a young preacher one thing always troubled me. Why did faithful, hard-working preachers – men who'd spent years studying the Bible and worked hard to understand the text as God meant it to be understood – see such little fruit? While there were other preachers who pulled verses out of context or, in a forty-five minute sermon hardly even opened the Bible, yet spoke with lots of passion and humour and enthusiasm, and their churches were full. I couldn't understand it. And then a friend of mine told me the answer, 'God blesses faith not correct exegesis.' And then I understood. It wasn't confusing after all, it wasn't a grey area. It was black and white. The big churches are run by men of faith and the little ones by men who lacked faith.

But then I met a few of the pastors of the big churches and the faith they exercised didn't seem as great as some of the faith I'd seen in the lives of the other pastors. And I went to work overseas and I met the most faithful, godly people of my life and they all saw little fruit. I couldn't understand it. But then another friend of mine explained it to me, 'Most of the people in the big churches are skin-deep Christians. These big churches just have revolving front doors; people come, stay a year or two and move on. The faithful pastors may have fewer numbers but they're quality Christians.' And then I understood. It wasn't confusing, it wasn't a grey area. It was black and white. Faithless preachers produce shallow Christians and faithful ones mature Christians.

But then I met some of the people from these big churches and they were mature, faithful Christians, prayerful and generous. And I met some of the people from the smaller churches and their lives seemed to hardly have been touched by the gospel.

So, what's the end of the matter? What do I conclude? It's this, the last words of Ecclesiastes: 'Fear God and keep his commandments.' For me it's simply to honour the Lord in my ministry: to prepare each talk diligently, faithfully, prayerfully, fearfully, rejecting any manipulative, underhanded methods, knowing I will have to render account for every word I've spoken – and doubly so if it's been the Word of God. For God will bring every deed into judgment. That day will reveal the true and the faithful. Until then I avoid trite answers; I don't feel the need to tie up every loose end, I simply leave God to be God, the Creator and Judge, and get on with living faithfully and wisely.

Youth and Old Age

by Chris Sinkinson

Chris has been involved in local church-based ministry in Canterbury and Bournemouth. He is now pastor of Alderholt Chapel near Salisbury. Having studied theology at Bristol University, he is now part of the teaching team at Moorlands College. His interests in Bible history have motivated him to lead a number of tours to Israel and to be part of an archaeological dig in Galilee. Chris has recently published a book on apologetics with IVP, *Confident Christianity*. He is married to Ros and they have two sons.

Youth and Old Age: Ecclesiastes 11:7 – 12:8

Where do you consider yourself on that spectrum between youth and old age? We have all met eighteen-year-olds who seem ready to retire and eighty-year-olds who seem in the prime of their youth. Your age depends on your attitude.

Trying to make sense of my own position in life, I came across various definitions of middle age. Middle age is 'when everything starts to click – your legs, your back and your elbows'. Middle age is 'when you are faced with two temptations and you choose the one which gets you home by 9.30pm'. Middle age is 'when you are told to slow down by the doctor, not the policeman'.

It has been pointed out that there are three ages of man: the age when you believe in Father Christmas, the age when you dress up as Father Christmas and the age when you look like Father Christmas.

Wherever you locate yourself on the passage of time from youth to old age, one thing is clear: you are older now than when you began. Time waits for no man. In the passage before us we find the emphasis on youth in chapter 11 and upon old age in chapter 12.

Enjoy life

Let's start with a simple and liberating command of Scripture: enjoy life! After all, it is good to be alive: 'Light is sweet, and it pleases the eyes to see the sun' (11:7). Don't we know the truth of this verse? The British weather is sometimes called variable, but it is more accurately described as wet! A couple of months of almost solid downpour remind us just how much light is sweet and the sun brings delight to the heart.

We have to be careful with figurative language in the Bible that we don't start reading things in that are not there. But I don't think we need to be reluctant to see a figurative significance to the images in this section of Ecclesiastes. The writer uses them to great effect and provides plenty of clues to enable us to spot them. Light and sunshine are pictures of life, while the darkness of verse 8 is a picture of death. The world is beautiful. It is good to be alive. Even in the rain or the chill of a cold starry night, life is sweet and a precious gift for us. What are we supposed to do with this gift of life? Verse 8 says, 'However many years anyone may live, let them enjoy them all.'

There is an ominous reference to darkness and meaninglessness that is going to be picked up in chapter 12. But we should pause for a moment on this appeal to enjoy life. Maybe some of you need to hear this. You carry a lot of burdens, worries and stress right now. And nothing I say is going to take those problems away. But enjoy life while you can. Enjoy today. Enjoy now. Don't let the worries of tomorrow rob you of your pleasure today.

Verse 9: 'You who are young, be happy while you are young, and let your heart give you joy in the days of your youth. Follow the ways of your heart and whatever your eyes see.' This is the scriptural equivalent of *carpe diem* – seize the day. Make the most of every opportunity. Stop wishing you were some other age than you are! Enjoying life while we can is a scriptural teaching but it's not one we often hear in church. After all, it's a teaching easily abused. It could sound like hedonism: 'If it's pleasurable, do it.' We warn our young people not to let their hearts rule their heads. We will qualify this teaching in a moment. But first, just enjoy this teaching for what it is.

The Bible commands us to enjoy life. Youth is a gift, make the most of it. Make the most of the fact that you are surrounded by opportunities: travel, ambition, friendship, discovery, learning new things and taking risks. God has created a world of great beauty. What dreams do you have? Be extravagant, be creative, change your routines. Make something, learn something new, go somewhere you have never been! What's really stopping you learning a new language? Why not try out that new gym down the road?

It doesn't have to be expensive. Enjoy your garden. Don't just see it as a chore. Don't cut the grass. Instead, watch the wild flowers that will emerge. Enjoy a free display of nature! And if you must cut the grass then enjoy that too. Grass grows because it is alive. You can cut the grass because you are alive! There will come a time when you will wish you still had the strength to cut grass. And if you don't have a garden, just stick a seed in a plant pot and enjoy watching what happens.

Sin is not just keeping out of trouble, it is also failing to enjoy God's gifts. Notice the enthusiasm that runs through these verses. Enjoy the pleasure of sight and what you can see (verse 7). Enjoy the passing days and the pleasure of change (verse 8). Enjoy the things that bring happiness (verse 9). Stop feeling guilty about the idea that you can be happy in this life. The teacher of Ecclesiastes encourages you to seize life by the horns and ride it wherever it carries you!

Now the reason we don't often hear this kind of teaching is because we assume a close connection between pleasure and sin. It would seem dangerous to enjoy what 'pleases the eyes' (verse 7), or 'follow the ways of your heart and whatever your eyes see' (verse 9). Isn't this a recipe for disaster? This is the reason for an early Jewish debate over the inclusion of this book in Scripture. These words could directly contradict Numbers 15:39: 'Remember all the commands of the Lord, that you may obey them and not prostitute yourselves by chasing after the lusts of your own hearts and eyes.'

But pleasure and obedience can be perfect partners. There is nothing wrong with pleasure and beauty; the problem lies within us. Our hearts are drawn to the wrong things for the wrong reasons at the wrong time and in the wrong way. It is not pleasure that's wrong, it's what we find pleasure in.

The right perspective on pleasure is given by the teacher: 'But know that for all these things God will bring you into judgment' (verse 9). We are accountable for our lives. We enjoy all good things in the light of our accountability to God. St Augustine famously said, 'Love God and do whatever you like,' the idea being that if you love God then you would want to do what is good and right. Maybe the teacher of Ecclesiastes would put it a little differently: 'Fear God and do whatever you like.' In the light of God our Judge before whom we will one day give an account, we may enjoy life as a wonderful gift.

Verse 10: 'So then, banish anxiety from your heart and cast off the troubles of your body. For youth and vigour are meaningless.' Young people are prone to depression. Anxiety robs us of living in the now. It is such a sad thing. Someone in the prime of their life, seventeen or eighteen, all their roads before them, and they are paralysed by depression. An eighteen-year-old fails an exam and thinks that his or her life has caved in. That's the sad thing about anxiety. It causes us to lose perspective. If you consider yourself young here and you fail an exam this summer, or lose a university place, or don't get a job, let me tell you there are hundreds of older people around you who can't even remember what exams they passed, let alone what exams they failed. Life moves on like a fast-flowing river; enjoy the ride, even when you hit the rapids! You'll be surprised how inconsequential those things will seem.

Now that's the point at the end of verse 10, 'Youth and vigour are meaningless.' Remember what we have been learning about this key word *hebel*. The Hebrew word is not a value judgment like 'meaningless' could otherwise imply. It is not intended as a negative valuation of youth. It is a statement of fact. It means something like vapour, steam, smoke. A parallel passage in Psalm 39:5–6 makes this clear in the similar way it uses this thought. We could read verse 10 as, 'Youth and vigour are so brief.' Like a light wind or breath, it passes away quickly leaving nothing behind. Don't get anxious about things. Most of what worries you is trivial. And those things that are not trivial, worry cannot help with!

Expect eternity

The next section turns from youth to old age and even to death. This may seem a bit of a morose theme. But, you know, a Christian needs to be able to look death in the eyes. Death holds no fear for us. Death is no awkward taboo in Scripture. Instead, it is a shadow that causes us to number our days aright: 'Remember your Creator in the days of your youth, before the days of trouble come' (12:1).

At last! Here is the key to a life worth living. A life worth living is a life lived in the light of the Creator. I think it is intriguing that the teacher does not use the word for God here, but the description *Creator*. He is saying: remember where you have come from, remember who made you.

Of course, in the Bible, the word 'remember' doesn't just mean 'keep a reminder'. It means to call something to mind in order to act upon it. It should make a difference to how we live our lives now. Don't waste your life: remember your Creator while you are young, and he will teach you to make the most of your life.

What follows in chapter 12:1–7 is an extended description of what is introduced as the 'days of trouble'. These are the days of old age and decline. This section is a poetic insight into the process of aging. And it is here in Scripture to remind us of what we do have. In the light of old age, we should delight in the relative health and youth that we do have.

Verse 1 introduces this figurative imagery of growing old by describing a point where we can no longer find pleasure in life. A tipping point is reached when physically life can no longer bring pleasure. Instead of the light, sunshine and pleasure of 11:7, we now have the darkness, rain and gloom of 12:2. Verse 2 is not describing changing weather. It describes failing eyesight. Not only the sun, the moon, the stars, but light itself cannot be seen. And that sets the tone for this chapter. It's a body in decline.

Verse 3 says, 'The keepers of the house tremble.' The house is a metaphor for the body. The keepers of the house are all those elements that keep our body alive and active. There comes a time in life when the house of our body trembles. Look at what follows. Verse 3b: 'the strong men stoop' – our muscles decay, the legs buckle, and the back bends. You see something lying on the floor and think twice about picking it up because it now seems an awful long way down and you aren't sure you can get back up again!

'The grinders cease because they are few' (verse 3b). Women would grind corn in the ancient Israelite house, just like teeth grind food in the mouth. But as time wears on, our teeth fall out and eventually, with few grinders left, eating itself becomes a chore. Where once we would have relished a steak in a peppercorn sauce, we now think twice about it. Someone offers us a toffee and for us it has become a calculated risk. All that delightful but unhealthy food we avoided in our youth we can no longer chew or digest.

The eyesight fails: 'Those looking through the windows grow dim' (verse 3), and our other senses begin to close down. Verse 4: 'When the doors to the street are closed,' may imply either the lips or the ears that fail. We either find it hard to hear or hard to be heard. Either way, we feel closed off from the streets outside. In old age we can sit at a busy dinner table with chattering friends all around us, but we cannot hear or be heard. The doors to the street have closed.

You know how in teenage years you cannot get out of bed until midday? And then with jobs, responsibilities or children you spend the next four decades longing for that day when you can have a lie-in again. Well, then comes a time when the jobs, responsibilities or children have all gone. You have the gift of a lie-in again. You could stay in bed until midday every day if you wanted to. But you don't. Verse 4 describes this time, 'when people rise up at the sound of the birds'. Why? Because you need the bathroom. As dawn breaks, at the sound of the birds, you rise because you need the loo. You might hope to enjoy the early morning dawn chorus of the birds. Not a chance. You can't even hear the birds (verse 4): 'All their songs grow faint.' You get up with the dawn chorus, but it isn't the sound of the birds that's waking you up, it's just that you need the bathroom.

And it gets worse. With age comes a fear of risk (verse 5): 'When people are afraid of heights and of dangers in the streets.' Children climb. They climb up trees, on roofs, over fences. As we get older we take fewer risks; even changing a light bulb becomes a major planning event. Wouldn't you have taken more risks when you were younger, knowing what you know now?

The description of the declining body continues with metaphors easily understood by an ancient Israelite. The blossom of the almond tree is white like the hair of the elderly (verse 5). The sight of 'the grasshopper' that 'drags itself along' is the insect at the end of the season. The grasshopper is spent. It has eaten too much, it may have lost a limb, that terrific spring seen at the beginning of the season is now replaced by the sad sight of its decline. Summer is over and the broken frame of the grasshopper is beyond repair. The mention of 'desire' that is 'no longer stirred' (verse 5) is a reference to the caperberry, an aphrodisiac in the ancient world. Its effects are felt no more. Desire is no longer stirred.

And then, finally, we meet images for death, when people go to their eternal home. A very wealthy person in the ancient world might have a candle lamp hung from the ceiling of their home. Light from a golden bowl would illuminate the room, attached by a silver cord. You would have to be very wealthy to have a light like that. But what about one day when the cord snaps and the golden bowl is smashed? It doesn't matter how much it cost. It doesn't matter what was spent on plastic surgery, private healthcare, hair dyes, false teeth, implants or extracts. When it is broken it has no value at all.

The bucket at a well, perhaps with a pulley on a wheel, is also broken and shattered (verse 6). It is not drawing water any longer. So verse 8 summarizes these broken domestic objects with the familiar refrain of the book; substitute the phrase 'passing away' for 'meaningless' and read this judgment: '"Passing away! Passing away!" says the Teacher, "Everything is passing away!"'

Now some of you are saying, 'I wish I hadn't come tonight. What a miserable sermon!' But it isn't. This book reminds you of the facts. You must know these things so that you can do something about it. What to do? Verse 7 provides the profound theological outlook on death: 'The dust returns to the ground it came from, and the spirit returns to God who gave it.' Life under the sun is brief, like vapour, here for a moment and gone. But, when we remember our Creator, we know from where we came and to where we are going. Youth passes swiftly. Old age brings regrets. But faith knows who made us and to whom we shall return.

You may be elderly and in poor health. You may be young and full of boundless energy. Either way, remember this: it is all vapour, passing away and temporary. Wherever you are on the spectrum from youth to old age, it is meaningless. It will not last. Everything will pass. But live life, not in the light of death, but in the light of eternity, and say triumphantly with Scripture, '"Where, O death, is your victory? Where, O death, is your sting?" The sting of death is sin, and the power of sin is the law. But thanks be to God! He gives us the victory through our Lord Jesus Christ' (1 Corinthians 15:55–57).

Be Sure

by Dominic Smart

Dominic is the Minister at Gilcomston South Church in Aberdeen. As well as speaking at conferences, churches and universities, Dominic has written several books, works with Langham Preaching and has been involved in the Faraday Institute's 'Test of Faith' programme. Dominic is married to Marjorie and they have four children.

Be Sure – The Wedding Feast: Luke 14:1, 7–24

Now here's a little comment from the heart of a speaker: there are times when your heart is full, your mind is full and your notes are full and, as Steve put it a few moments ago, it's like you've got a whole oceanful of stuff and a thimble to put it in. That's how it is this evening. There is just so much in this passage. It is full to overflowing with joy, with gladness and with greatness. It's full of the greatness of the love, the lavish generosity and the open heart of God. Our hearts should be full of the loving-kindness of our God who, with nobody making him do it – that is just because he wants to – invites you and me, sinners as we are, to his great eternal feast, to his great wedding feast. Tonight's passage is immeasurably glorious.

A number of themes orbit round this passage or, if you prefer, like sparks from a Catherine wheel are flung out from this passage. And I want to mention them before we begin to look at the details of the text, just so that we've got it in our minds what it is we're going to be seeing. Sometimes a little bit of a prequel helps you; sometimes if you watch a trailer for a movie it helps you get something that is going on in the movie; you just make more sense of it.

This day, that day

So, in no particular order, here are five themes. First, do you remember on Sunday evening we mentioned Martin Luther's calendar? Martin Luther said he only had two dates on his calendar, two days – *this day*, today, and *that day*, the day when the King comes in all his glory. Now in this passage, particularly verses 15–24 which is the parable of the great banquet with many guests invited, all three sections of this chapter absolutely cement in our minds that as far as Jesus was concerned, never mind Martin Luther, there are really only two days – *this day* and *that day. This day* is the day for decision which will affect what happens to you on *that day. This day* is what determines, in a sense, the outcome of *that day. This day* is a day for closing with Jesus, receiving him, believing in him so that on *that day* you are welcomed into his eternal kingdom and not left on the outside where there is weeping and wailing and gnashing of teeth.

And in these parables the importance of *this day* and *that day* is crystal clear, because there is an earthly banquet and there is a heavenly banquet. Jesus is at the earthly banquet. It was the Sabbath, Saturday, and he was in the house of a prominent Pharisee – not insignificant as we will see. Jesus takes what is happening on *this day* and speaks about what will happen on *that day*. He's not laying out some sort of detailed order of events for the last times so that we can fit it into a systematic theology book. He's precisely not doing that because the whole focus is on just the two days: *this day*, when he is here, how will you respond to him? And *that day* when your response will be fixed forever. Now that's the thinking that's going on in this chapter, two days – *this day, that day* – two banquets: the one that Jesus is at on the Sabbath in the house of a prominent Pharisee, and that great banquet when he returns, that great last day feast, that great wedding feast of the kingdom of God.

Kingdom values revealed

The second thing that is going on is what the boffins call the eschatological reversal. Eschatology is the last things: death, judgment, heaven and hell. It is the coming of the kingdom in all its fullness, the coming of the King in all his glory, when every eye will see him, every knee will bow and every tongue confess. The day when he will come in all his glory and receive his people to himself and take them to be with the Father forever; the day when he comes and judges in all his glory; the day when the fullness of his kingship, which is now and already but we don't see it all yet, is revealed for everyone to see. That's the eschatology bit. It's not just a long word that the boffins use and it's not just a set of arguments that Christians have. It is our Lord

Jesus in all the fullness of his glory returning and receiving that which is his due and that which every Christian heart longs for him to have, wants him to have, sees that he should have: that is, all praise and honour and glory and dominion and power for him, given to him, acknowledged as being his. And on that day a huge reversal will be revealed.

It's going on all the time, but it's going to be revealed then. So what looks great in the kingdom of this world will be revealed as awful in the kingdom of God in all its fullness. Exaltation in the kingdom of this world will be massive downgrading in the kingdom of our God. Success in the kingdom of this world, gain in the kingdom of this world, will be loss in the kingdom of God when it comes in all its fullness. So on the day when, as we read in Revelation, the kingdom of this world has become the kingdom of our God and of his Christ, the humble will be lifted up, the weak will be made strong, the downtrodden will be raised, all the values of this world will be turned upside down. There are hints of that now – there should be in the life of the church – and that's what's being talked about in the passage this evening.

U-shaped seating plan

The third thing that is orbiting around this passage is the distinction of the clean and unclean. Jesus is in the house of a prominent Pharisee. The Pharisee knew absolutely and for certain from God, from God's Word, from all the history, from all the historical development of the rules and regulations that were added to what Moses had written – he knew who was clean and who was unclean. He knew that the unclean could not go near God who is pure, only the clean could, and he would make sure that he was one of the clean. Amongst the unclean, there would be the crippled, the lame, the blind, and those who lived outside the nice little Jewish community, the Gentiles. None of them would stand a chance of tasting anything at the great final banquet that the prophet had spoken about, that the rabbis had taught about, that every good Jew was aching for. The unclean wouldn't stand a chance of getting there; they would not taste it, they wouldn't get in. Whereas the clean, who kept the rules, the clean, who made themselves clean by their works, the clean, who really had scored enough points with God, they would get in.

And the better they were with the rule-keeping, the closer they would get to sit to the Messiah. There was a U-shaped seating plan. The Master of the banquet, the host, the King, sits in the centre of the bottom of the U and the most important seats are on his right and on his left. The important guests are seated next to the King at the banquet and then the lesser guests, the lesser and lesser until you're at third cousin twice removed who, you can guarantee, won't get on with anybody else.

A great party

The fourth thing is that the kingdom of God, when it comes in all its glory, is good. I don't just mean morally good, I mean it is just so immeasurably fantastic that it makes everything else pale into insignificance. Why do you think when Jesus is talking about the kingdom coming in all its fullness, why do you think he describes it as a wedding feast, a great party? Because that's what people would understand as being a) a massively significant occasion, b) a wonderfully lavish occasion, and c) something that would involve a really good meal which everybody enjoys even if they pretend they don't. A party is terrific in terms of the company, the *craic*, the dancing and all the rest of it. *Craic* is an Irish term for conversation; it's nothing to do with medication! Everyone has a real blast at these things, that's the idea, that's what people would understand by this and this is not insignificant. And I'm not just saying this because I'm a Yorkshireman, but it was a blast at somebody else's expense. In a few moments we will celebrate communion; it will be bread and wine; it'll be a body broken and blood shed. It is a celebration at somebody else's expense.

Be humble

So how do these things come together? Well, the first thing is that Jesus watches people take their seats. He notices exactly what happens in the world; he notices people jockeying for position, and he notices people going for proximity to power. They want to be near the person who seems the most influential; they want to be near the host; they want to be near, in this case, the prominent Pharisee. And because Jesus notices everything, he notices the guests picking for themselves places of honour at the table (verse 7). So Jesus explains that in the kingdom of God you don't do that. He says when somebody invites you to a wedding feast you don't take the place of honour because you might end up getting relegated, which is really humiliating. Instead you choose somewhere near the top of the U-shaped seating because then, when the host arrives, he might see you sitting there and think, 'No.' And in front of everybody he'll say, 'Come, sit close here,' and that will feel really, really good. You'll be glad you were there.

But, of course, when Jesus starts to talk about a host doing that, when Jesus picks up points that we find in the Old Testament in the book of Proverbs, that we find elsewhere in the New Testament, even in Luke's Gospel (Luke 8:14, 20:46–7), Matthew's Gospel (Matthew 18:4, 23:12) and 1 Peter 5:6, he's making the point, 'Look, in my kingdom if you humble yourself you'll be exalted, if you exalt yourself you'll be humbled.' Now what's going on there? It's not simply, 'Be humble.' What Jesus is doing is staking his claim to give honour. You are honoured by the host, the master of the feast, the king, the person who's throwing the banquet, the person who paid the price – he gets to choose who and what is honourable in his house, at the feast that he has paid for. You don't get to choose that for yourself, you don't get to claim that for yourself. Jesus said, 'That's for me to confer and I will confer it with a completely different set of values from the one that this world uses.' Be humble, not simply in terms of choosing your seating, so to speak, but be humble and let Jesus do with your life what he will. Don't seek the limelight, don't seek proximity to power, don't drop names about who you know and who you don't know. Some of the ones you say you know will be quite surprised to learn you know them! Don't tell everybody your track record; just be humble; let Jesus honour you as and when and how he chooses.

Be kind

Then the point builds a little in the next section in verses 12–14. And here we have another reversal going on and it's the reversal that takes place over this question of clean and unclean. 'Jesus said to his host, "When you give a luncheon or a dinner, do not invite (just) your friends."' You see the point that there is a worldly generosity which is not generosity at all, it's actually bargaining; you're buying, you're not giving. It's like when you give your cash to the person at the till at Tesco, that is not a donation, you're buying. Jesus says, 'Do not invite your friends, your brothers or sisters, your relatives, or your rich neighbours; if you do, they may invite you back.' You say, 'Well, that's the idea, isn't it?'

Jesus said that when you give a banquet invite the poor, the crippled, the lame and the blind. Now the poor were just socially outcast, but the crippled, the lame and the blind were to the prominent Pharisee and all the other sycophantic people, unclean. They wouldn't want to touch them in case they contaminated themselves and they became unclean. The unclean could not go near God and they certainly would never have a place in the great eschatological feast, the great wedding of the King, the feast of the kingdom.

And then Jesus says, 'When you give a banquet invite these very people and you will be blessed. Although they cannot repay you, you will be repaid at the resurrection of the righteous. Do the right thing on *this day*, do the kingdom thing on *this day*, do the thing that Jesus would do on *this day* and on *that day* you will gain the benefit' (author's translation).

Jesus asserts his right to decide who will be at his feast and on what terms. People won't be there because they have kept themselves right according to somebody's rules. They won't be there through self-righteousness; they will be there by invitation. They will be there because Jesus wants them there. Jesus completely assumes the right, the power and the authority to make people clean. Jesus can make you clean; you can't, I can't, your pastor or vicar can't; reading good books won't make you clean. Trying to keep the rules won't make you clean, so by the Pharisee's score you have no chance of being there. But Jesus can make you clean and pure and he welcomes you into the banquet.

Be sure you'll be there

The first major bit says *be humble*, and the second major bit says *be kind*, because that counts in the kingdom; God can make people clean. Then the third bit says *be sure that you'll be there.* And how do you make sure that you are going to be there? By not refusing the invitation. The pattern was that the wedding invitations would go out and people would accept them. Then all the preparations would be made for the feast and when the feast was ready a second announcement would go out. It wasn't really an invitation; a second announcement would go out saying the feast is ready. You've said yes, you're coming; you've been invited, come along in now, and at that point the excuses start to flow, don't they? They all began to make excuses.

In verse 18, 'The first said, "I've bought a field, and I must go and see it."' You think, is it going to disappear or something? What is this? It's a field; they don't, generally speaking, go away overnight. A feeble excuse. 'Another said, "I have just bought five yoke of oxen, and I'm on my way to try them out"' (verse 19). You could do that tomorrow, couldn't you? I mean, five yolk of oxen, they're not going to disappear overnight either. And the third one said, 'I just got married, so I can't come' (verse 20).

None of you, I think – well, one or two of you – would have heard of Herbert Silverwood who was a lay preacher in the West Riding of Yorkshire when I was a lad. Herbert Silverwood was preaching on this passage and said, 'That's enough to make a cat laugh. What woman doesn't like to go to a wedding?' The only problem was in terms of the exegesis of the passage. In those days women, generally speaking, didn't get to go to a wedding feast because it went on for a long time, well into the night, when people would get tired and you couldn't guarantee the gentlemanliness of the behaviour. So it was actually quite normal for a wife not to go to a wedding feast. Still a feeble excuse, isn't it?

And look what happens: surprise, surprise, the unclean are invited – the poor, the crippled, the blind and the lame (verse 21). And the Gentiles, those who are staying outside the nice little Jewish community, go and get them as well; I want my banquet full. Notice two things: it's an echo of what's going on with the healing in verses 2–6. Jesus is going to do the kingdom thing, the massive lavish generosity, the huge invitations, and great welcome. The feast is going to happen anyway; by not being there you are not going to stop it happening. It's no use saying, 'I'm going to take my custom elsewhere;' it's going to happen, the feast is going to happen, the King is going to come, he's going to have the banquet hall full. Jesus says, 'I'll have the poor and the crippled and the lame and the blind, all the ones that you called unclean, I'll make them clean and I'll have the Gentiles that you despise, because I love them too. This is a feast for all nations.'

Now if the point is *be there and be sure you're going to be there*, and if this is part of Luke's Gospel, and this is part of Jesus' preaching of the kingdom, then, when you and I speak the Word of God in the midst of a crooked and depraved generation, shining like stars in the universe, when we make disciples of all nations, when we preach repentance for the forgiveness of sins in Jesus' name, this is what we've got to say; it's what Jesus said. You are invited to heaven. Jesus wants you. He doesn't have to have you; he invites you because he wants to; no one's making him, he really wants you. And not only are you invited but you're not being invited because you think you're good enough, you're being invited because Jesus wants you and he can make you good enough. You're not going to get in because you've kept some rules and you've been religious for a while, you get in because the King wants you in. All you need to do is to receive the gift of this eternal life from the King; you can't earn it, you can't buy it, you don't deserve it – none of us do – Jesus just gives it, and what he has in store makes the very best of this world look cheap, niggardly and hollow by comparison. Be sure that you will be there; I mean that this evening. If you're not sure, be sure that you will be there by saying, 'Yes,' to Jesus who even now is inviting you to come into his eternal home. And when you go out with the gospel, don't go out with the gospel which just says, 'Jesus can tweak your life and make you happy now,' go out with the gospel which says, 'Jesus wants you and he wants you forever.' Will you come to him?

Be Committed

by Calisto Odede

Calisto is Senior Pastor of Nairobi Pentecostal Church. He worked with the Fellowship of Christian Unions with students in universities and colleges for thirteen years, including pioneering and directing the Commission Conference, a major students' missions conference in Africa. He then served with IFES for eight years. Calisto has travelled to many countries conducting Bible exposition and leadership training. Calisto is married to Elizabeth and they have three sons.

Be Committed – The Tower: Luke 14:25–33

A number of years ago I used to work in the Sudan. And two young men, both of them Muslim university students, got together without any invitation from a Christian, to spend time reading the Bible and the Koran and comparing the two books. This went on for one or two months. In the third month one of them, called Mohammed, came to the conclusion that the Bible was actually true and he cast doubts on the Koran. When this happened, his friend, whom he had been reading the Bible with, went and reported him to his parents. His parents warned him that if he did not change what he was saying about the Bible and the Koran they would disown him and hand him over to the religious police, whose responsibility it was to take care of Muslims who converted to Christianity.

Mohammed didn't change his views. So the parents decided that the best thing was for him to get married to a Muslim girl who knew the Koran and who would influence him to change his mind. The girl began interacting with Mohammed and within two weeks she had become a Christian! At that the parents were so angry they handed him over to the security police. This man took Mohammed and spent a week or two torturing him – removing his nails with pliers and forcing him to sign documentation saying that he would no longer associate with Christians. After he signed the documentation they released him. He quickly looked for one of our leaders and they kept him hidden for one and a half years. And it was during that time I met Mohammed. I held his hands and prayed with him, encouraging him that God is a father to the fatherless. But as I prayed with him a question came to my mind, 'What is it that can make a young man in his sober mind go through such torture, such rejection, including rejection by his own parents?' And I came to the conclusion that it can only happen when the reality of the Lord Jesus Christ is so convincing to an individual that he becomes thoroughly committed to Christ. This is the kind of commitment that you and I are being called to; it is the kind of commitment that every believer needs to give their lives to; it is the kind of commitment that may make you go in an opposite direction to your entire family, the kind of commitment that will make you cross boundary lines, seas and oceans in order to be able to proclaim the Word of God.

A radical commitment

And so we turn to the parable in Luke 14:25–35 as we reflect on the call that Christ gave to all of us. First of all, in verses 25–26 we are called to commitment to Christ; if I may say so, commitment to a person. Jesus seemed to be a spoil-sport. His words were not the kind of words that you use if you want to influence people and win friends. Dr Luke, the physician, tells us a great crowd is following Jesus. This was the kind of crowd that any itinerant preacher would have loved to have walking by his side and following him; it would show his popularity; it would show how great he was, how majestic he was, and yet that is the very same moment that Jesus chooses to drop the bombshell.

We are not told why the crowd was following Jesus. Perhaps they had seen and heard about his miracles, perhaps he had fed them when they were hungry, perhaps they were enchanted by his teaching or perhaps they had a mistaken notion that he was going to establish his kingdom and chase away the colonizing Romans, or maybe they were just curious to see him. For whatever reason they followed him and, instead of welcoming them and appreciating them for coming, instead of patting them on the back and saying, 'You have done well to come after me', he turns to them and says, 'Um, um, that's not the thing. If anyone comes after me, follows me, and does not hate his own father and mother and wife and children, and brothers and sisters and yes, even his own life, he cannot be my disciple' (author's translation).

One of the things we are amazed to understand when we read this parable is how this call would have appeared to a Jew. Some of us don't remember the last time we saw our parents; we don't care about them; they can do what they want, and we have no idea where they are. But for a Jew not to show honour and respect to your parents meant you were actually cutting your life short; you would not live your full life. For Jesus to say they must hate their parents, immediately there would be a repugnant feeling in their hearts and they would say, 'No, no, no, that's not the right kind of teaching. No-one should hate their parents.'

I still remember preaching on this passage more than twenty-two years ago and an old man walked over to me and he told me, 'You teach them to hate their relatives but me, I teach them to love their relatives.' Now this dear old man had it all wrong, because he missed the point that I was trying to make. The Good News translation tries to blunt the edge of this statement by giving us a more acceptable understanding. It tends to say those who come to me cannot be my disciples unless they love me more than they love their mother, wife, children, brothers and sisters and themselves as well. Although we must conclude that the word 'hate' in verse 26 is rather strong and can only be a hyperbole, an extension of a truth or a figure of speech that is meant to communicate something, yet we must also come to the conclusion that what Jesus is laying down is, 'I must be above anyone else, above anything else in your life if you are to be truly committed to me.' And that cannot happen unless he's real to you.

There's got to come that point when he ceases to be just a name written on the page of a book; there's got to come that point when he's no longer just a word that you hear from the mouth of the preacher; there's got to come that point when he's no longer just a name that we occasionally mention in our songs; there's got to come that point when you know from the very depth of your heart that Jesus is real and say, 'I am committed to him because he is alive, he is real and it is worth being committed to him.'

That's radical commitment. It is commitment to the end; it is moving from the modern-day brand of Christianity where people are moving with the crowd and with popular opinion; it is knowing that sometimes your family values may demand you live in a way that contradicts the way Jesus is calling you to, and that automatically you will go to the way that Jesus says. No, it is not the double standards or lies that we find in modern-day Christendom, it is true commitment to Jesus Christ.

Sometimes I get amazed by some of the things that are going on in Christian circles. Not too long ago some armed thugs raided a bank in Nairobi, the city in Kenya. They went to the bank very early in the morning and captured the guards who were guarding the bank with guns, tied them up and locked them in a room. They put on the clothes of these guards and, as the workers reported in, one after another, these thugs would take them to the room and lock them up. Finally the manager came; they got him to open the safe, they took the money and they locked him up also. In Nairobi we have all these office fellowships, and in the morning sometimes you hear people singing. And the strange thing was as these thugs were locking up the people in the bank they were singing a Christian chorus. They sang 'Come, come and be part of the flock of the Lord Jesus Christ.' Imagine singing thugs? Worshipping thugs who are raising their hands, singing and giving glory to God as they are robbing you at gunpoint! That's not commitment. We may not be thugs, but maybe the lifestyles and certain values we espouse automatically show that Jesus is not real to us. So Jesus states the truth clearly for them and us: 'If you do not hate your parents, if you do not hate your wife and your children, if you do not hate your brothers and your sisters, you cannot be my disciples. I am above all else, you've got to put me above everything else' (author's translation).

Some of us might say, 'That's great; that's very easy for me; after all I don't like my siblings or my wife. Great idea! That's OK for me.' No, Christ was calling us to express deep devotion to him that would lead us to his purpose and his agenda. It included a willingness to give up our lives, that we would count our lives worth nothing compared to the excellency of knowing him and espousing him in our lives.

In 1844 the CMS missionary, Ludwig Krapf, was able to establish a mission station in my own country in Mombasa, Kenya. He came to Mombasa when there was not even a single Christian in Kenya. Two months later he was bereaved by the death of his wife and his only child. He wrote back to his sending agency CMS in those memorable and moving words:

> Tell our friends that there is on the East African coast a lonely grave of a member of the Mission cause connected with your Society. This is a sign that you have commenced the struggle with this part of the world; and as the victories of the church are gained by stepping over the graves of many of her members, you may be the more convinced that the hour is at hand when you are summoned to the conversion of Africa from its eastern shore.[1]

What could have made him stay after losing his wife, after losing his only child? Many other missionaries came to Africa. Those days of mission work were cut short by malaria. These missionaries knew they would die. Some of them packed their clothes in their coffin knowing that a little while later their bodies would be shipped back in those coffins. What made them do that? Commitment – commitment to the Lord Jesus Christ.

Carrying Christ's cross

Not only did Jesus call his listeners to a radical commitment to him, he called them, of all the things, to carry the cross. In verse 27 Jesus says, 'Whoever does not carry his own cross and come after me cannot be my disciple' (NASB). 'Please, Jesus, another call, something less demanding.' The cross was not something anybody would celebrate about. It was not carrying a bag full of accolades, it certainly was not a medal, the cross was not an achievement – it was repugnant. Bearing the cross was done publicly. The condemned individual, whether a defeated rebel, an ordinary criminal or a thief, carried the cross and marched on the streets with everyone watching. It was a repugnant idea, it was a shameful idea. Everyone who watched would know, 'There goes a criminal, there goes a thief, there goes someone who has done something wrong.' It was public and shameful.

It was a painful venture because everyone who carried a cross knew they were making a terminal journey. They were not going to come back; that was their final journey. They were going to be crucified, a very torturous and painful death, and so carrying the cross was a fatal journey. And yet Jesus turns to this great crowd and multitude that is following him and he tells them, 'Whoever does not carry his cross and follow me cannot be my disciple' (author's translation).

He could tell them that because he knew in a few weeks' time he would be walking to Golgotha carrying his own cross. So he was not telling them a mirage or a false statement; granted, he did not mean that people would literally carry a cross that they would walk around with on their shoulders, but it did mean that people were to come to decisions and to walk a lifestyle where they were willing to be crucified on a daily basis for the sake of the Lord Jesus Christ. It did mean that they would be making decisions that were cross-like in their lives. For some of them it may have meant ridicule; for some of them it may have meant being ostracized from their families; for some of them it may have meant giving up things that they cherished. You see, the cross speaks of suffering; the cross speaks of hardship; the cross makes radical demands upon us; the cross says give your all. That is the call upon our lives.

And, even tonight, that same call is resounding down the corridor of your soul, down the corridor of your heart, down the corridor of your mind, urging you: 'You cannot be my disciple unless you carry my cross.' It may mean for some of you you've got to give up your career. It may mean you've got to begin thinking whether you really should go into that retirement home or whether you should get involved in mission work somewhere. And for all of you who are above eighty you are just getting ready to be used of the Lord! That's where Moses was when God appeared to him in the backside of the desert. He was exactly eighty and he received his energizing call to go and lead Israel into the Promised Land. And so none of us are exempt, regardless of our age; the Lord is still urging us and saying, 'Carry your cross and follow me in the direction that I would lead you, the way I would map out for you.'

Kiss goodbye

Thirdly, Jesus urged them to count the cost in verses 28–33. He used two metaphors to show that the kind of commitment he required of them was to be well thought out and complete, commitment where they would give their all to the Lord Jesus Christ. And so he used the metaphor of constructing a tower. He told the people to think of an individual who wants to construct a high-rise building, a tower. Before he can make the decision to construct the tower he sits down and comes up with a budget. And as he looks at his budget he asks, 'Am I, with the money that is available, able to complete the tower?' If he is not able to complete it then he will not begin the project. Jesus explained that if he goes on with the project but does not complete it then people will begin laughing at him. 'See this man here, he started that work but was unable to complete it; he did not count the cost of building and constructing.' The parable is urging us to take seriously, to sit and think through, the cost of following the Lord Jesus Christ and responding to his call. There are a number of us who would use this parable as an excuse for not responding to God.

I like talking with young people. You ask them, 'What is the Lord doing in your life? What are you thinking about?' And they would say, 'I'm waiting on the Lord.' The next year you meet them and you say, 'So how is the Lord treating you; what is going on in your life?' 'I'm waiting on the Lord; I've been waiting on him.' And there are many people who have been waiting on the Lord for the last eighteen years. They're still waiting on the Lord. Now that is not what Jesus is telling us. Jesus is telling us to take significant count of what the cost will be in terms of following him. He is not telling us to abandon commitment to him because we won't be able to afford it. That's not what he's telling us and so we cannot use that as an excuse at all.

But he uses a second metaphor, the metaphor of war, or conquest, in verses 31–33. In this parable he sees a military commander who must first sit down and consider his military strength. He sees his opponent coming against him with a military might that he cannot match. He has three options: to win a victory, to be destroyed by his opponent, or to ask for a truce. This decision has got to be made because either way the opponent is coming. And so although the parable of the tower seems to suggest that you sit down and count, you can't sit down and count forever. The opponent is coming and you've got to come to a decision and a conclusion on the way forward rather than keeping on waiting and waiting. It is only then when you come to the decision, 'I will make truce, I will come in peace, I will surrender, I will yield, I will give in,' that finally you truly make a commitment to the Lord Jesus Christ.

Listen to how Eugene Peterson in *The Message* puts it: 'Simply put, if you are not willing to take what is dearest to you, whether plans or people, and kiss it goodbye, you can't be my disciple' (Luke 14:33). We need to be willing to kiss goodbye to plans or people. There are some of us here in wrong relationships and you need to come to that point and say, 'I'm going to cut it off; I'm going to cut it off.' There may be some of us here that have issues in life, baggage you are carrying that you know you need to roll off your shoulders tonight and say, 'Have your way in my life, Lord; I'm going to cut it off, I'm going to kiss it goodbye.' Commitment is to give our all to the Lord Jesus

Christ. It is to surrender, it is to let go, it is to say, 'Lord, you are my Lord, take over my life, take over my future, take over the direction of where you want me to go.' God is calling us to give our everything. Surrender and yield to him.

Notes

1. Ludwig Krapf, quoting from the *Church Missionary Papers*, CXXXIII (CMS, Lady Day 1849).

Jesus Is Coming Soon

by Ian Coffey

Ian is Vice Principal and Director of Leadership Training for Moorlands College. Married to Ruth, they have four adult sons and three granddaughters. Having led churches in several contexts they are now involved in training a new generation for servant leadership, speaking at conferences around the world. Ian has published fourteen books, and Keswick is a special place for Ian and Ruth – as they first met here forty-one years ago!

Jesus Is Coming Soon: Revelation 22:8–21

Tonight we come to the last words not just in the book of Revelation, but in the Bible. And if you want a verse that sums up the theme this evening, I think verse 20 would be very appropriate: 'He who testifies to these things says, "Yes, I am coming soon."'

One of the sad things in recent years in the church of the Lord Jesus, particularly in the United Kingdom, is that we talk so little about the second coming. Now there are reasons for this and if we had time this evening it might be good to explore the reasons. I think sometimes preachers steer away from the theme because of its abuse and misuse in the past. But so many of God's people, in different parts of the world and in different times in history, have found the truth about the return of the Lord Jesus to be a great encouragement and a stimulation to action.

Many of us will have heard of Lord Shaftesbury. The iconic image of Eros in the middle of Piccadilly Circus was erected by the people of London to thank God for that Christian man who put his faith into practice and championed the cause of the poor and marginalized. Lord Shaftesbury was driven by this thought that one day the Lord Jesus would either call him home or would return. Those who studied his life say he knew he'd been given responsibility and was accountable before God, and what caused him to take up these big issues of the poor, the marginalized, those who had mental illness, children who worked in factories, was the sense that Jesus was coming back. And, apparently, those close to him say he used to wake in the morning and before he started the day he would ask God the question, 'Perhaps today Lord? Perhaps today?'

Tonight we look at this climax of history, the coronation of our Lord Jesus Christ. And here, as John gets to the end of this great revelation, this amazing experience he encountered, notice he talks about the purpose of this revelation in verse 6: I, Jesus, have sent my angel to give you this testimony for the churches. John realized that this revelation entrusted to him wasn't some private spiritual experience that he could talk to his children and grandchildren about. It was a revelation for the churches, the church in every age and every generation, that we might be encouraged and strengthened to know that history is heading towards an end point.

Notice in verse 17 the invitation that is open to all: 'Whoever is thirsty, let him come; and whoever wishes, let him take the free gift of the water of life.' Our God is an evangelist from the very beginning of Scripture to the end; he always wants to reveal himself to those who do not yet know him. What an invitation that is! And then in verse 20 you can feel the sense of anticipation: 'He who testifies to these things says, "Yes, I am coming soon." Amen. Come, Lord Jesus.' It's one of the oldest Christian prayers in 1 Corinthians 16: *Maranatha*, Come, Lord Jesus. And we echo that from our hearts, don't we? When we read the news and see the pictures on our television screens, when some of us struggle with the sense of loss and bereavement in our own lives, we look at our world and long for something better. Our hearts cry out, 'Yes, come; come, Lord Jesus.'

But I want you to notice in these verses, these last sentences in the book of Revelation, there are three warnings, three exhortations, three encouragements that frame, not only tonight as we break bread, but our footsteps as we leave Keswick and go home. As you go back to that difficult church situation, as you go back into that work situation where you are the only believer in the whole of your department, how should we walk?

Avoid distraction

Here's the first warning: it's a warning against distraction. Did you notice in verses 8–9 John hears these things and then falls down to worship at the feet of the angel who'd been showing them to him? The angel first comes in chapter

1:1 and then again in 21:9 and 22:1. There's reference to this angel showing John what's happening, and you realize that for John this was an amazing experience. He'd never known anything like it before, and so with a sense of wonder and awe of all that he had seen, he falls down at the feet of this angelic messenger in an act of worship. What does the angel do? The angel says, 'Do not do it. I am a fellow servant with you and your brothers and the prophets of all who keep the words of this book. Worship God' (verse 9). The angel says, don't worship me, don't be distracted, worship him – 'the Alpha, and the Omega, the First and the Last, the Beginning and the End' (22:13). Friends, the warning that we have here is to make sure that our focus is not in any sense captivated or sidetracked by the wrong thing. It's possible for you and me to become distracted, even about good things and godly things.

I teach in a theological college and in the college a fight broke out, literally a fistfight between two students. Their fellow students managed to pull them apart and when they sat in front of a staff member who said, 'What on earth caused this to happen?' Do you know what the argument was about? They had differing views on theories of sanctification! Jesus called it straining at gnats and swallowing camels, majoring on minors (Matthew 23:24).

I remember having a heated debate one day with a church member about church furniture. And I said to him, 'Let me ask you one question: when we get to heaven will the Lord Jesus ask us about where we put this table?' And he said, 'No, he won't', and so I said, 'Let's not worry about it now. If it's not going to be an issue then it shouldn't be an issue now.' And, friends, we can be distracted about translations of the Bible, about methods of church governments, mode of baptism, whether we celebrate the Lord's Supper, the Lord's Table or the Breaking of Bread, the Eucharist, Holy Communion. We can major on minors, make mountains out of molehills and become distracted. We can draw lines of separation from sisters and brothers in Christ with whom we need to be working in partnership. We can make a thing out of worship. We can make a thing out of preaching and particular methods of preaching. These are meant to be things that lead us to love Jesus more and serve Jesus better. Beware of becoming distracted.

Live clean in a dirty world

The second warning is about dirt. Look at verse 14: 'Blessed are those who wash their robes, that they may have the right to the tree of life and may go through the gates into the city. Outside are the dogs, those who practise magic arts, the sexually immoral, the murderers, the idolaters, and everyone who loves and practises falsehood.' Why is the word 'dogs' used? Because in the Bible the word 'dog' is a symbol of things that are impure, that are unclean. If you look back to Revelation 7, we read about those who have washed their robes and made them white in the blood of the Lamb. The tense in the Greek language is the aorist, denoting a 'once-for-all' action. When you trust the Lord Jesus your sins are forgiven, they are wiped away, they're blotted out and your name is entered into the Lamb's book of life. But here in 22:14 the word 'wash' is in the present tense: it's not to do with our salvation but that daily cleansing that you and I need. Keeping short accounts with God, cleansing for when you spoke that hasty word, for today when I was unkind in my response and selfish in my attitude. That sense of the Lord Jesus' imminent return encourages us to keep short accounts with God and with one another.

In verse 15, 'outside' doesn't necessarily mean that they are there at the doors of the heavenly Jerusalem. It's the sense that the unrighteous are not part of this. The list of sinful practices is not exhaustive, but you get the idea. John is talking about unrighteousness and unrighteous living. And the message, friends, that you and I are to take home with us is this: we're called to live clean in a dirty world.

All around us there's the pull of the world to follow this kind of attitude, to live this sort of lifestyle. But we're called to live differently: we're called to live righteously. Hear what I say very carefully: the Bible doesn't call us to live self-righteously but to live righteously, not a pharisaic self-righteousness that looks down on other people and has a 'holier than thou' attitude to life. You know the sort of folk who feel that godliness means having a miserable countenance, the sort of people who take the swing out of the budgie's cage on a Sunday, just in case. The Bible calls us not to self-righteousness but the kind of righteousness that Jesus had. One of the things that challenges me continually is the way in which the Lord Jesus, holy as he was, attracted sinful people. What was the criticism? He hangs around with all the wrong people; he hangs around with the drunkards, with the gluttons, with the immoral. What was it about Jesus that created in these people a hunger? What was it about him that was so magnetic? It was the sense that they weren't written off, they weren't looked down on. There was no element of self-righteousness that said how holy I am and how inferior you are. Jesus lived clean in a dirty world and people were drawn to him, and that's the call for you and for me to live clean in a dirty world.

Let me remind you of what the Hebrew writer said. Hebrews 12:1–2: 'Therefore, since we are surrounded by such a great cloud of witnesses, let us throw off everything that hinders and the sin that so easily entangles, and let us run with perseverance the race marked out for us. Let us fix our eyes on Jesus, the author and perfecter of our faith.' How do we go the distance? We go the distance by throwing off anything that hinders, by getting rid of the sin that so easily entangles. And, friends, I don't know about you, but for me that's a daily business, a constant business. Let's run and go the distance with our eyes fixed on Jesus. Beware of distraction, beware of dirt and, thirdly, beware of deception.

Look out for deception

Did you notice 22:18–19? 'I warn everyone who hears the words of the prophecy of this book: If anyone adds anything to them, God will add to him the plagues described in this book. And if anyone takes words away from this book of prophecy, God will take away from him his share in the tree of life and in the holy city, which are described in this book.' Many preachers have found that a pretty intimidating warning. John Calvin, who wrote a commentary on every book of the Bible, would not write a commentary on Revelation because of that warning. You can't play with it; you are not allowed to tamper with it; it's God's Word and we are warned about deception.

Turn with me to 1 John 4:1–3. The apostle John, the same apostle who had this extraordinary revelation of God, writes to the people of God, 'Dear friends, do not believe every spirit, but test the spirits to see whether they are from God, because many false prophets have gone out into the world.' Do you believe that's relevant for today? Of course it is. 'This is how you can recognize the Spirit of God: Every spirit that acknowledges that Jesus Christ has come in the flesh is from God, but every spirit that does not acknowledge Jesus is not from God. This is the spirit of the antichrist, which you have heard is coming and even now is already in the world.'

John says many false prophets have gone out into the world and that's why, friends, we need to know our Bible. We need to have an intimate relationship with God, Father, Son and Spirit, through Scripture. And we need to know our history, understand the story of the church, what God has been doing in different generations and ages. It doesn't mean we become hypersensitive and look for heresy around every corner, but we need to be men and women of maturity, men and women of deep understanding like the men of Issachar who understood the times and knew what Israel should do (1 Chronicles 12:32).

Be aware of distraction, be aware of dirt and stay clean in a dirty world, and watch out for deception. Jesus is coming, so how are you living? How am I going back from Keswick into my world? What are the things I am going to be carrying with me? What are the things that God has said into my life? If I used the name Alfred Nobel, immediately you'd think of the peace prize. Alfred Nobel and the story of the peace prize is fascinating. Nobel was a Swedish industrialist; he made himself a very wealthy man, but his money came primarily from the invention of TNT, dynamite. Now he developed TNT primarily for engineering, for building roads, railways, bridges and tunnels. But inevitably human nature as it is, people took a good invention and used it in a destructive way. One morning he came down to breakfast. He knew that his brother had died, but when he opened the newspaper someone in the newspaper office had pulled the wrong pre-prepared obituary out of the file, and he read his own obituary instead of his brother's. To his horror he realized how the world would remember him: as a man who made his fortune from misery, destruction and death. And he made a very important decision, that he wanted to change the way he lived and the way that he would be remembered. So he took his massive fortune and he put it into trust funds with the decree that after his death five prizes would be awarded each year in the realm of physics, chemistry, biology, literature and peace. He was fifty-five when he read that obituary and he died eight years later, but he changed the course of his life, values, attitudes and legacy. And my question to you is, what life course adjustments are you and I going to make in the light of what God has done in our lives at Keswick 2012?

John very kindly prayed for me before I came up to speak and talked about my preparation for this message. He didn't realize, but I had a very strange preparation for this message four weeks ago when we as a family took part in a sponsored walk. I have a nephew, a guy called Phil Coffey, who's a lovely guy with some big life challenges. We wanted to do something to express our love and commitment to him in a practical need that he faces. And so we decided to do a 30-mile walk in one day along a valley which runs from Salisbury Cathedral right down to where Moorlands College is in Christchurch. Because of the floods most of the track was washed away, and so at the last minute we had a change of plan and decided to walk along the coast for 30 miles. I hadn't planned that to be my sermon preparation for going the distance, but trust me, it was. We walked 30 miles in 10 hours and 55 minutes and, you know, I learned two important lessons.

Fellowship and focus

First, the importance of fellowship: six of us in the family did it and doing it together made it possible. We supported one another, there was humour and leg-pulling, and those little words of encouragement we needed. And we made it because of each other. Hebrews 10:25 says, 'Let us not give up meeting together, as some are in the habit of doing, but let us encourage one another – and all the more as you see the Day approaching.' How do we keep going? How do we go the distance? We need one another; don't neglect to meet together. You know the attitude which says, 'Well, I'll be there on Sunday if it's not raining,' or 'I'll come if there's nothing better that comes into the diary.' That's consumer Christianity. But I need you and you need me.

Some of you remember the ministry of the late David Watson. I remember David saying once at a conference that an enthusiastic preacher was teaching how in the body of Christ we need one another. And he said, 'I want you to turn to the person you are sitting next to and say to them, "I cannot live without you."'. David Watson said, 'I was sitting next to this stunning blonde that I'd never met in my life before, hoping that no one from my church was there as I said, "I can't live without you"'! But, friends, it's true. I can't live without you! And you can't live without me. Don't neglect to meet together as some are in the habit of doing, 'and all the more as you see the Day approaching'. It was a first-century problem, and in the same sense it's a twenty-first-century problem.

What was the second thing I needed? Focus. When we walked that coastal path it had stopped raining and we thanked the Lord for that, but the gale force winds had started to blow. We were walking into a westerly wind, and as the day went on the wind got stronger and the sand began to blow up from the beach into our faces, and our eyes, our noses and our hair. How did we keep going? Focus. Why were we doing it? We were doing it for Phil. What was the purpose? That we might encourage him, let him know that he was loved, and to raise some much-needed funds for a practical need. We kept the focus clear. And as the Hebrew writer said, 'Let us fix our eyes on Jesus.' Don't look at your church, loved as they are by God, because often it can be a discouragement. Don't look at that fellow Christian who's stopped running the race; love them and pray for them to get back into it, but don't be distracted and let your vision wander. Fix your eyes on Jesus and he will enable you to go the distance.

Do you see the very last word in the book of Revelation? It's there in verse 21. It's a wonderful ending; it simply says, 'The grace of the Lord Jesus be with God's people.' As you go home from Keswick, whatever you face, God's grace is with you. You don't leave it behind here; it's not something you stock up on and wait till next year when you get replenishment. God's grace is sufficient for everything that you face. Embrace the fellowship of God's people and maintain that focus with your eyes fixed on Jesus. Run well and run to the end. Amen.

Keswick 2012

Keswick Convention 2012 teaching is available now
All Bible readings and talks recorded at Keswick 2012, including Simon Manchester, Steve Brady, Jeremy McQuoid, Ian Coffey, Christopher Ash, John Risbridger, Peter Maiden, Michael Baughen, Calisto Odede, Dominic Smart, Mike Raiter and Chris Sinkinson are available now on CD, DVD*, MP3 download and USB stick from www.essentialchristian.com/keswick.

Keswick teaching available as an MP3 download
Just select the MP3 option on the teaching you want, and after paying at the checkout your computer will receive the teaching MP3 download – now you can listen to teaching on the go: on your iPod, MP3 player or even your mobile phone.

Over fifty years of Keswick teaching all in one place
Visit www.essentialchristian.com/keswick to browse Keswick Convention Bible teaching as far back as 1957! You can also browse albums by worship leaders and artists who have performed at Keswick, including Stuart Townend, Keith & Kristyn Getty, plus Keswick Live albums and the *Precious Moments* collection of DVDs.

To order, visit www.essentialchristian.com/keswick or call 0845 607 1672.

*Not all talks are available on DVD.

Keswick Ministries

Keswick Ministries is committed to the deepening of the spiritual life in individuals and church communities through the careful exposition and application of Scripture, seeking to encourage the following:

Lordship of Christ – to encourage submission to the Lordship of Christ in personal and corporate living
Life Transformation – to encourage a dependency upon the indwelling and fullness of the Holy Spirit for life transformation and effective living
Evangelism and Mission – to provoke a strong commitment to the breadth of evangelism and mission in the British Isles and worldwide
Discipleship – to stimulate the discipling and training of people of all ages in godliness, service and sacrificial living
Unity – to provide a practical demonstration of evangelical unity

Keswick Ministries is committed to achieving its aims by:

- providing Bible-based training courses for youth workers and young people (via Root 66) and Bible Weeks for Christians of all backgrounds who want to develop their skills and learn more
- promoting the use of books, DVDs, CDs and downloads so that Keswick's teaching ministry is brought to a wider audience at home and abroad

- producing TV and radio programmes so that superb Bible talks can be broadcast to you at home
- publishing up-to-date details of Keswick's exciting news and events on our website so that you can access material and purchase Keswick products on-line
- publicizing Bible teaching events in the UK and overseas so that Christians of all ages are encouraged to attend 'Keswick' meetings closer to home and grow in their faith
- putting the residential accommodation of the Convention Centre at the disposal of churches, youth groups, Christian organizations and many others, at very reasonable rates, for holidays and outdoor activities in a stunning location

If you'd like more details please look at our website (www.keswickministries.org) or contact the Keswick Ministries office by post, email or telephone as given below.

Keswick Ministries
Convention Centre
Skiddaw Street
Keswick
Cumbria CA12 4BY

***Tel*: 017687 80075; *Fax*: 017687 75276**
***email*: info@keswickministries.org**

Keswick 2013

Week 1: 13th – 19th July
Week 2: 20th – 26th July
Week 3: 27th July – 2nd August

The annual Keswick Convention takes place in the heart of the English Lake District, an area of outstanding national beauty. It offers an unparalleled opportunity to listen to gifted Bible exposition, meet Christians from all over the world and enjoy the grandeur of God's creation. Each of the three weeks has a series of morning Bible readings, and then a varied programme of seminars, lectures, prayer meetings, concerts and other events throughout the day, with evening meetings that combine worship and teaching. There is also a full programme for children and young people, with a programme for young adults during each week. Prospects will again be running a series of meetings for those with learning difficulties in Week 2. There will be a special track for the Deaf in Week 3, along with Keswick Unconventional, an opportunity to explore more creative and imaginative aspects of Christian spirituality.

The theme for Keswick 2013 is
The Transforming Trinity – Knowing the Triune God.

The Bible readings will be given by:
Charles Price (Week 1)
John Lennox (Week 2)
Steve Gaukroger (Week 3)

Other confirmed speakers are Richard Condie, Peter Baker, Paul Mallard, Rico Tice, Mike Hill and Paul Williams.*

* Speakers' list correct at time of going to press. Check out the website for further details.

NEW TITLE

The Transforming Trinity

Knowing the Triune God

A study guide
by Elizabeth McQuoid

The word 'Trinity' is never mentioned in the Bible. And yet evidence for one God in three persons is found throughout the Scriptures. In this study we will find out why the Trinity is central to our beliefs and fundamental to the working out of our faith. We will never exhaust the riches of the Trinity – it is a mystery. But as we grow in our understanding of God, we will learn to worship him more fully, reflect his image more clearly and experience his transforming power in our lives.

The first in our range of Bible study resources for individuals and small groups available at Keswick 2013

The Amazing Cross

by Jeremy & Elizabeth McQuoid

ISBN: 978–1–84474–587–6

The cross of Christ is the heartbeat of Christianity. It is a place of pain and horror, wonder and beauty, all at the same time. It is the place where our sin collided gloriously with God's grace.

But do we really understand what the cross is all about? Or are we so caught up in the peripherals of the faith that we have forgotten the core?

The authors present us with a contemporary challenge to place all of our lives, every thought, word and deed, under the shadow of the amazing cross, and allow that cross to transform us here and now.